The Library Byelaws and Regulations apply to the loan of this book. It should be returned or renewed on or before the latest date stamped below. Items may be renewed three times only by post or telephone at any library.

M.W. Moss, M.A., F.L.A., Borough Librarian

PLEASE BRING YOUR TICKET TO THE LIBRARY EVERY TIME YOU BORROW OR RENEW

Greenford Library
Oldfield Lane South
Greenford, Mx
UB6 9LG
Tel. 0181-578 1466

Water damage YB.

20. FEB. 1999

-8. JUN. 1999   28. JUN 2000   2 8 JUN 2003

-9. FEB. 2000   26 July oo   2 8 AUG 2003

23. MAR. 2000 15. FEB. 2001   -9 MAR 2004

-7. JUN. 2000   -1 JUL 2004

                  2 3 NOV 2002   2 7 APR 2005

                  1 5 MAY 2003   0 9 JUN 2005

FINES ARE CHARGED FOR RETENTION BEYOND THIS DATE   LIB.38.7/95

About Storytelling

A PRACTICAL GUIDE

Storytelling

HELEN McKAY & BERICE DUDLEY

HALE
& IREMONGER

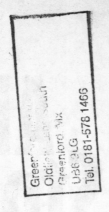

© 1996 Helen McKay and Berice Dudley

First edition
10 9 8 7 6 5 4 3 2 1

Typeset by
DOCUPRO, Sydney

Printed & bound by
Southwood Press Pty Ltd
80–92 Chapel St, Marrickville, NSW

For the publisher
Hale & Iremonger Pty Limited
GPO Box 2552, Sydney, NSW

ISBN 0 86806 593 5

National Library of Australia
Cataloguing-in-Publication

McKay, Helen, 1937– .
  About storytelling.

  Bibliography
  Includes index.
  ISBN 0 86806 593 5.

  1. Storytelling. 2. Storytelling—Handbooks, manuals, etc.
  I. Dudley, Berice, 1931– . II. Title.

808.543

Contents

Acknowledgements

THE authors wish to thank all the people who have assisted them to write this book. Your efforts are much appreciated.

Special thanks go to Mary Locke who read our drafts and kept us on track, to Ken McKay for not mowing the lawn while we were writing and who helped at the computer instead, and to Diane Wolkstein, master storyteller, who critiqued our work and gave us helpful information.

Thank you also to the authors who generously allowed us to use some brief quotes from their books.

Also thanks to other members of the Storytelling Guilds of Australia for their encouragement.

Special thanks to the Chinese Takeaway in Toongabbie who saved us from a lot of cooking and freed us to do our writing.

About Storytelling

> 'Each of us has been designed for one of
> two immortal functions, as either a
> storyteller or as a cross-legged listener to
> tales of wonder, love and daring. When
> we cease to tell or listen, then we no
> longer exist as a people. Dead men tell
> no tales.'
>
> — from *A Recipe for Dreaming*
> by Bryce Courtenay

THIS book is for storytellers, teachers and speakers, or anyone who has a message to offer or a tale to tell. It is suitable for beginners, or more experienced tellers — anyone who wishes to enhance their storytelling skills and improve their style.

We wrote this book because so many people from diverse backgrounds asked at our workshop presentations for an up-to-date book about storytelling, relevant to Australian audiences and conditions. Unable to satisfy their request with the name of a recently published Australian book, we decided to write what we have learned and experienced about storytelling.

Currently there seems to be an upsurge of interest in story-telling, both in Australia and internationally. We have noticed there is a demand by our audiences for a connection with 'real people' instead of the canned or impersonal images filtered through machines such as videos, television and films, with their violence, explicit sex and lack of moral values.

Because of the changes brought about by the electronic media, especially television, video and, more recently, CD ROM programs, people are now becoming accustomed to superficial five-minute grabs of information. As a consequence of this we find the attention span of many people in our audiences has been reduced. In the book we attempt to show storytellers some ways to regain and hold their audience's attention.

We show how storytelling is both an art form and a craft: an oral form of painting pictures with words, that is, pictures in the minds of the listeners. Both the teller and the audience can interact with each other to share and co-create a vision — a vision of the story unfolding as it is told.

We also show how story, one of the oldest forms of the healing arts, has the power to repair damaged feelings, give insights, restore lives and build bridges to reunite our communities. The power of a storyteller, or the magic of a story should never be under-estimated.

We have included a comprehensive bibliography for those who wish to find out more about storytelling. Many of the books listed have helped us and will help you to develop and polish your skills.

Storytelling is a living art and therefore needs to be nurtured carefully as you would a plant. Feed it by finding out as much as you can about the skills you can use and the stories you tell. That way you will experience as much satisfaction as your audiences.

1 What's Storytelling?

*'Stories belong to the spiritual heritage
and popular humour of the human race.'*
— from *The Prayer of the Frog*
by Anthony de Mello

WE are all part of a story — a life story. Part of a continuum with links that began with the arrival of human existence on earth and which will go on through our descendants far into the future.

Storytelling is recognised as one of the earliest forms of human activity. 'Tell us a story' (along with 'I love you' and 'Pass the dinosaur bones') would have been among the first words uttered by the human race.

Early people were not concerned with literature and art as such, but were driven by the basic need to survive. Stories began in caves. There were no books, radio, or television back then. To a group of cave-dwellers huddled around a campfire, a teller of the stories of hunts and battles would be highly prized and in great demand.

Early cave paintings and drawings, precursors of the written word were possibly the illustrations of early man's spiritual  beliefs. It has been suggested that the stories and drawings of the hunt were an attempt to establish a spiritual relationship with the animals portrayed in the hope that they would materialise in great numbers and so ensure an abundant food supply.

The earliest written stories were recorded 4000 years ago by ancient Sumerians on cuneiform clay tablets. About this time Egyptians carved their stories on their temples. Around 1200 BC, papyrus, a form of paper was made from reeds and used to record stories.

But many races have no written history. Their stories were handed down from generation to generation by tribal storytellers, elected by the people as narrators and curators of the traditional tales. They were gifted people who held an important place in those early societies.

In recent times many of these traditional stories have been lost because they were not recorded in a written form. There is now a race on among anthropologists to find and rescue these tales before they are lost forever.

Traditionally, Australian Aboriginal wisdom, stories and culture were handed down orally. Because of the breakdown and dispersal of tribal communities even some of these are in danger of being lost forever.

In working with Aboriginal groups, we have become very aware of the deep sense of community loss caused by the fractured connection with their culture. Because it was government policy to separate Aboriginal children from their parents some years ago, many have grown up with no knowledge whatsoever of their ancient tribal stories or culture. Fortunately, the universal wisdom in these stories is now becoming recognised and valued across many cultures.

William Ricketts, an Australian anthropologist who lived in the Dandenong Ranges in Victoria, worked hard during his life to rescue and preserve some of the Aboriginal stories and culture.

Jennifer Isaacs, author of *Australian Dreaming, Wandjuk Marika* and other books on Aboriginal culture and customs, also seeks to rescue the knowledge so it can be passed on to later generations. *Yorro Yorro*, written by David Mowaljarlai and Jutta

Malnic, explains some spiritual beliefs and many Aboriginal customs. Fortunately, communities in Australia and throughout the world are attempting to record this precious knowledge and set it down in print.

What is a story?

A story is defined as a narrative or tale of real or fictitious events. Stories are a nourishment for our hungry souls. Often stories we regard as fiction have elements of truth dressed up to make them more palatable. Stories are magic, taking us everywhere: backwards, forwards or happening right in the present time, transporting us to many places and situations we might never go.

The teller is the magician, creating an atmosphere in which anything is possible. Storytelling, presented well, develops a special kind of energy between the teller and the audience — it really is magic.

Telling stories is like taking a group of people to the cinema. You can think of storytelling as a piece of film being projected on to a screen. The vision of the script writer and director are what the audience sees and interprets.

In a similar way the storyteller shows the pictures seen in his or her mind and passes them to the listeners' minds for interpretation. Each time the story is told the words change, according to the way the teller visualises the images passing through his or her mind. The teller tailors the story to suit that particular audience.

Storytelling works much like driving a car — the story is made up of a basic three-act structure. The teller prepares the audience (turns the key and puts the car into gear), lets out the clutch, so the audience (car) picks up speed and, with each gear change, they travel together along a story (road). The magic is in each individual's 'journey' or connection with the teller and story.

Similar to a journey in a car, each person's enjoyment is different. Some notice every detail along the way, while others, only focus on major aspects of the journey, such as the technical details of the drive. So it is with storytelling.

Is there a difference between written and 'told' stories?

Written versions of stories are not the same as oral ones. Reading restricts the teller much more. The text is an outline of what the teller sees, but the language is in a different (literary) shape or form. The storyteller frees up the static language and gives it life and form.

The story-reader has to find a way to compensate for the loss of the storyteller's accoutrements: body language, eye contact, intonation and natural pace. This loss may necessitate some modification to the language to speed up the action. Illustrations can help, but again, they are someone else's interpretation of the teller's vision.

Stories entertain, inspire, instruct and heal. They are as relevant now as they ever were. Stories are like onions. There is the surface skin and then there are the many layers of sub-text that need to be peeled away before you come to the heart or wisdom of the stories.

There are many different types of stories. The most important consideration when choosing a tale to tell is whether you like it enough to tell it with enthusiasm. Stories should communicate to you a need to be told.

Some of the different categories of stories available to story-tellers are:

1. *Fable* — a short moral story not based on fact, using animals as characters, such as, Aesop's Fables — 'The Fox and the Grapes', 'The Hare and the Tortoise' and others.
2. *Fairytale* — the best-known would be Grimm's fairytales about imaginary folk, such as elves, giants, witches, gnomes,

and fairies. Closer to home is *Mary and the Leprechaun*, by Irish-Australian writer John Kelly.

3. *Folk tale* — a traditional story, in which ordinary people gain special insight, transforming them and enabling them to overcome extraordinary obstacles. See *The Magic Orange Tree & Other Haitian Folktales* by Diane Wolkstein.

4. *Legend* — a story based on the life of a real person in which events are depicted larger than life, for example, *The Stories of Robin Hood,* or *King Arthur and the Knights of the Round Table*.

5. *Myth* — a story about gods and heroes, explaining the workings of nature and human nature. See *Psyche and Eros* or *Inanna* by Diane Wolkstein.

6. *Parable* — a fictitious story told to point to a moral, for example, *The Sower and the Seed* from the New Testament of the Bible.

7. *Personal story* — a life story from your own or your family's experience, such as, *Streets and Alleys* by Syd Lieberman.

8. *Religious story* — an historical and philosophical story based on a particular culture and religious persuasion, for example, *The Story of Lazarus* from the Bible.

9. *Tall tale* — an exaggerated story, often humorous. Fishing stories, Australian bush stories, see 'The Loaded Dog' by Henry Lawson.

10. *Traditional tale* — a story handed down orally from generation to generation, such as the Polynesian stories — *Maui,* and *The Coming of the Maori*.

Anyone with a message to convey can do so more memorably and effectively with an appropriate story.

A really good spinner of yarns, especially one who 'doesn't let the truth get in the way of a good story', adds spice to any barbecue, pub-drinking school, or family get-together. They use storytellers' licence (a variation of poetic licence) to rearrange a story and improve it.

Storytellers connect with, or engage their audiences in order to entertain, educate, heal and communicate. The stories they tell have a common thread — they contain universal truths — aspects of life with which we can identify. This, most of all, has meaning for all ages. Everyone's experience is different, so each member of the audience hearing a teller perform will leave with a different perception of the performance and with their special individual memories of other times rekindled.

Our uniquely human gift of language is the basic tool or medium used, although, there is some evidence of another unspoken connection — the psychic connection between audience and teller, as yet incompletely researched.

Storytelling is a living and flexible, or responsive, art for the story can be altered by the teller to suit the audience at each telling. The words of stories on paper are incomplete until storytellers speak them and, weaving their magic, bring them to life.

The storytelling presentation is the tale brought to life by a combination of the teller's personality, emotions, insights, and ability, plus the special feedback which comes from the audience and helps the teller to create magic with stories. It is essentially a sharing experience.

Professional speaking groups, such as the National Speakers Association of Australia, recognising the power of story, are now including sessions on the art of storytelling for their corporate members and trainers.

'Once upon a time . . .' is one of the most guaranteed attention-getting phrases of the English language. Everyone loves a story!

2   *The Room Set-up*

THE room set-up is of primary importance and should be considered well in advance. Try to arrange ahead for an inspection of the venue to make certain that the room set-up meets your requirements. If you or your audience is distracted by noise or movement in and out of a doorway, people passing by a window, or even by objects hung around the walls, your audience can quickly tune out and lose the thread of your story.

At the time you book your venue, discuss how you wish the room to be arranged. Make sure these factors are taken into consideration. If possible, rearrange your room and have any potential distractions removed. Your efforts will be rewarded by greater audience satisfaction.

If you are to do a presentation in a large auditorium, close off the back rows of seats so the audience fills up the front rows first. Release the closed seats only when those closer to you are full. Likewise, if you are to perform in a tiny enclosed space try not to speak with your back to the audience. Reorganise the seating if you can in order to allow everyone to see and hear you equally well.

We recently attended a storytelling in an old stable with a diamond-shaped space. The V-shaped bleachers were parallel to the performance space and created quite a few problems for the teller, noticeably restricting his movements to a very small area.

Often, the storyteller needs the audience to sit closer together to heighten the effects of drama in a story. Try to keep your audience tight so all their responses can be effectively shared. If they are in a badly organised room, adult audiences are loath to cry in public, or, at times, to even laugh at the funniest story.

It's amazing how well emotional responses can sweep through a carefully placed, bonded audience. In the past I've seen whole audiences weeping in emotional scenes, expressing anger about perceived wrong-doings and laughing infectiously at humorous spots — all in the one tale.

These effects can be intensified by carefully planning the seating of your audience. You want that response to humour to be infectious if you are telling a funny story. Seat the audience in such a way that when one person laughs at the comedy, their response triggers a similar response in the rest of them.

Have someone with you who can help you rearrange the seating to satisfy your needs and don't worry if the venue organisers are miffed about the changes you make. They are not giving the presentation. Think carefully about the layout you need and do check it out before you present your story. Avoid placing seats where pillars or pot plants block the audience's view of your performance.

Lighten up

Try to have uniform light throughout the room in which you are storytelling. There should not be a darkened audience and a very bright stage. The lights can be lowered and a carefully placed spotlight used, but make sure you are not positioned in front of a bright light, so that you appear to be in silhouette.

You and the audience need to see each other clearly so that you can comprehend the unspoken messages you send each other. This 'visual language' helps to regulate the speed of audience reactions to your story. When members of an audience and the teller are free to relate to each other, there will be an exchange and sharing of emotions. If the audience is remote from the teller and, worse still, seated out of sight of the teller and in the dark, that sharing is just not possible.

It is worth while taking some moments before you begin your story to set up that communication bond with the audience.

To break down barriers and build bonds among the audience, some of our friends get everyone to stand, shake hands and talk to each other before the presentation begins. Some even get them to form pairs and gently massage each other's shoulders. It's hard to remain distant from someone whose shoulders you've just touched.

Other presenters have special music playing to set the emotional tone. Maybe you can all sing the national anthem, a national song, such as 'Waltzing Matilda' or, at Christmas, a carol. Churches do this by having the congregation sing hymns prior to the sermon.

If you wish to bond closely with your audience, work closer to them and make your eye contact all-inclusive. Each person needs to feel you are talking directly to them. Get everybody involved by allowing them to participate with you — remember to include the people in the back rows.

Before you start your story, check to be sure everyone can hear you clearly and, during your performance, don't forget to make eye contact with them. In any audience interaction it is essential that you include the people in the back rows — don't allow them to feel excluded.

It's easier to get a successful shared response from a larger group than a small one. Storytelling to a larger audience, from forty people upwards, is like riding large ocean swells on which you can surf very smoothly and predictably. Emotion sweeps through them like waves.

Keep small groups seated close together and relate directly to them. Small audiences are like choppy waves, made up of a lot of individuals who bounce you around, making it difficult to ride.

When 'telling' to school groups try to limit the numbers to an absolute maximum of 200 children. Ideally school audiences should not include more than four consecutive grade levels and must always include teachers or parents, who can monitor and manage the students' behaviour. You are too busy telling the stories to be responsible for badly behaved, disruptive children.

Use that space

Some 'tellers' prefer to create space in which they and their audience can interact and move around. When you have allowed room in front for movement, make sure you use that space effectively. Exaggerate your movements if necessary, but use that space. Don't let it be viewed as a barrier between you and the audience.

If there is movement allowed for in your story, take it right in amongst the audience. Allow some of them to participate. You'll find people love to become involved.

Take care that everyone can clearly hear every word. If you speak while moving, some of the sound will be deflected and part of the audience will miss what you're saying. Let your audience hear you clearly. Remember: move — then speak; move again — then speak.

When working with puppets, get up and walk around allowing the audience to touch or stroke the puppets. That tactile experience is so important. Children love to feel the texture of things (as do adults) and you're guaranteed to become a winner by letting them touch a part of the story.

Consider the audience's needs

Berice and I once had the opportunity to tell stories to a group of forty sight-impaired teenagers. Some of them had a small amount of peripheral vision but the rest were mostly blind. With such an audience it was not practical to tell stories requiring good gestures or body language. Visual aids, such as pictures or other objects, would also have been ineffective.

After some discussion, we decided to present interactive stories and utilise as many auditory and tactile aids as we could. We used primitive musical instruments — such as rain-sticks, elephant drums, thumb cymbals, maracas — even a South American sitar. So each child could experience and touch something different, we took a huge basket of silver-painted pine cones to pass around at the end of the performance.

They enjoyed the interactive stories and the musical sounds we wove into our stories. When they received their pine cone, each person felt it all over, held it up to their nose and smelt it, then to their ear and listened to it. Finally, where some had a small amount of peripheral vision, they held it close to their eyes trying to see what it looked like. It was very humbling to see that the solution we'd found to accommodate their special needs made such a difference to their enjoyment.

Berice also took her huge bag of magical hand puppets for the young people to handle. For a while we were overwhelmed by eager teenage boys and girls, all wanting to try out the puppets and musical instruments. The evening was a total success and finished with us surrounded by very enthusiastic youngsters who were keen to know how, they too, could become storytellers.

Make sure you can be seen

If you are storytelling to a large audience made up of many rows of people and you cannot stand on a podium or stage which allows you to be seen easily, make sure any gestures you use come from shoulder height. Generally performers use gestures from elbow height or below, which risk being lost on anyone but the first few rows. Practise these shoulder-height gestures in a mirror until they seem natural and appropriate to the needs of the story when you have to use them.

Remember also, to keep the height of your puppets constant. *Puppets don't grow taller or shorter during a performance unless the story says so.*

Think carefully about the special needs of each audience and use the appropriate techniques to satisfy their requirements. Learn to share experiences with your audiences to enhance their enjoyment of your storytelling. Remember, these are the memories they take away with them; special memories which often last a lifetime.

14

3 *Beginnings*

> *'The White Rabbit put on his spectacles.*
> *"Where shall I begin, please your*
> *Majesty?" he asked.*
>
> *"Begin at the beginning," the King said,*
> *very gravely, "and go on till you come to*
> *the end: then stop." '*
>
> — from *Alice in Wonderland*
> by Lewis Carroll

GOOD beginnings are vital. Have you ever attended some kind of performance and, soon after the opening sentences, felt so switched-off you wished you could get up and walk out? The beginning was just a non-event, leaving you feeling disinterested and unsatisfied.

Whether your story is a private little 's' story, or a larger 'S' Performance Story, the beginning is one of the most significant components of your presentation. Together with the ending, the beginning defines its boundaries, creating a framework into which the body of the story fits. Begin with drama and end quickly with drama. A crisp lyrical opening will grab your audience's attention.

Stories begin some time before the performance or storytelling is to take place. They begin with the selection of a teller, an appropriate venue and an assortment of stories to suit that particular audience's needs. Not every story suits the teller's style or the target audience.

Careful selection of a suitable story is vital to its reception. You need to choose a story with sufficient 'pictures' in it to satisfy the needs of the listeners. Tailor it, being aware of unnecessary language or scenes which can be dropped. Try to dwell longer on other, more significant details which will advance the story's plot.

In the same way you'd bake a cake, you need to get the balance of ingredients right. Not every ingredient is beaten in — some are gently folded to retain the air which will keep the cake light and moist. So it is with storytelling.

What makes a good beginning?

Let's examine the beginning of your story. Look carefully at the first paragraph. Does it have a strong opening? Strong enough to hook the audience's interest? You can lose that attention so quickly if you have not done your homework.

If, during the preparation of your story, you feel it doesn't meet the listeners' needs, rework and reshape the words so they have a stronger impact and are more direct. You are telling the story and you alone know what outcome you are expecting.

Think of your storyline as a straight and narrow path from which you should not stray. You will soon lose your listeners' interest if you wander off into places and events that have little bearing on your story. The plot is your road map — use it.

The beginning should contain some knowledge of the time, information about the place, the main character and a sense of the adventure or story to come. Just as in fishing, you need to bait your hook well if you really want to catch your fish. A strong beginning is an irresistible lure.

When you are reworking the story, decide where in the piece *you* want to begin. Do you want a sequential story, starting at the beginning? Or, maybe you could begin at a dramatic high point, from which you could explain how the body of the story came to pass, finishing strongly with the crisis and resolution.

Your audience wants to sense the adventure ahead of them. Get them sitting bolt upright — as soon as you can — listening intently. If possible, have them sitting on the edge of their seats. The most beautifully worded descriptive scene is worthless if,

because of using it, you lose the interest of your audience. So
. . . analyse your story, decide where to start and go for it.

It is equally important that you know where and how you are
going to end. Begin and end strongly to give your audience a
satisfying experience.

Points to consider before beginning to tell a story

As suggested in the previous chapter don't be afraid to rearrange
the room to suit your needs and ensure your listeners' full
attention. Having decided the dynamics of the room layout, the
'teller' may wish to play some music prior to the performance.

This serves to divert the listeners from their external stresses
and bring them around to a more receptive state for your
storytelling. Such stresses as a frantic day, difficult interpersonal
relationships, a desperate dash through traffic to attend your
performance — complete with parking problems, can create
difficulties for you and impede their enjoyment of your performance.

Familiarity with the type of microphone you are
to use is very important. Some people prefer a
cordless lapel mike while others like to work with a
boom mike. Some prefer to hold the microphone in
their hand: others prefer to leave their hands free so
that they can concentrate on gestures.

*Discuss all these requirements well in advance with the person
who is booking your venue — especially if they are to provide
the sound equipment.*

We strongly urge you to arrive early. This allows plenty of
opportunity to change anything you find unsatisfactory about
your room set-up before your audience is seated and waiting for
you to begin.

If a meal is served, ask that the dishes are collected before or
after your presentation. Make certain that there will not be
distracting noises, such as clanging crockery or cutlery during

your presentation. Remember to make the arrangement *before* you are ready to begin speaking.

Your early arrival also lets you mix and develop some bonds with members of the audience, prior to the performance. This pays off handsomely: a part of your audience is already on your side before you have started to speak.

Make sure you have set up all the props, costumes and any other aids you require prior to starting. It's so easy to lose an audience if you are fumbling around looking for equipment during a performance. We've seen it happen! And . . . it is very hard work for the storyteller to try to regain that audience's attention. Many people in the audience will simply switch off completely.

Preparation is vital. It is your responsibility to check, check and recheck. You just can't get out there and hope for the best.

Before your audience arrives, check that your microphone is performing correctly. Always have spare batteries readily available.

Ensure there is a good supply of water handy (at room temperature), should you need to lubricate a dry throat, during your presentation.

Arrange with the audience about any parts they are to play before you begin telling the story. If there are responses, such as, audience interaction or choruses, write them up in easy-to-read print on a whiteboard, or prominently display them on a flip chart or overhead screen.

Now . . . at last . . . you are ready to begin! You are introduced and welcomed with applause. Allow the audience a pregnant pause, giving them time in which to settle. At this point we often begin with a simple trill on a sitar or similar sound.

Sometimes, we use another primitive instrument, such as a rain-stick, or even hand-clapping, finger clicking and foot stamping, to begin setting the scene. Pause again . . . then, with a deep breath, begin in a strong, clear voice, 'Once upon a time', or whatever the opening line of your story is to be.

While all this may seem overly dramatic, *you really need to build that bridge of time and drama to give your story a kick-start.*

All storytellers begin their performance differently, using any one of a variety of methods and rituals. *There is no one right way* — experiment to find out what works best for you.

A member of our group, Yuri, the Russian Storyteller, seats himself comfortably, opens his attaché case, lights the story candle and pauses momentarily. Taking a deep breath, he launches into the story, using his narrator's voice (one of many different voices). That process of lighting the candle concentrates, or focuses, his audience's attention.

Diane Wolkstein writes in her book, *The Magic Orange Tree*, that in Haiti storytellers wanting to tell a story, shout out 'Cric!' When someone in the audience answers with 'Crack!' the audience sits ready to hear the storyteller begin. If no-one answers with 'Crack' the story is declined and with another 'Cric' and 'Crack' the next teller takes over.

In other countries 'tellers' will use music or percussion instruments (such as bongo drums, or even song) to transport their audience from 'here and now' back to 'there and then'.

Some 'tellers' simply stand impassively, with hands clasped, until the room is settled. Then, with a deep breath, they begin: 'Once upon a time . . .'

The reason so many tales start out with that particular opening line is that the phrase transports the listener's mind into a different world, involving another reality — the world of story.

Having begun the story, it is essential that you follow that dramatic opening by using your voice, your eyes and maybe some gestures. Your audience is now hooked. It is up to you to reel them in with the storytelling which follows.

4 Linking with an Audience

THE audience is the critical third leg in the storyteller's stool: *the first leg* is the storyteller; *the second leg* is the story; *the third leg* is the audience. Ask any milkmaid how hard it is to sit on a stool with any of its legs wobbly or missing.

Your aim as a storyteller is to connect with your audience. To hook into their minds and emotions — to communicate. You are telling a story with words, but you are dealing with magic here — triggering and directing the audience's imagination. You are responsible for their experience.

Read your audience

The way in which stories are passed on is very important. They should not be rushed, but should be simply and carefully told, so the audience can visualise all the action. You and your audience are creating a vision together.

Look into their eyes, watch them closely, read their reactions, respond to their expectations. Your audience's body language will give you all the clues. Watch for these. Pace the story to suit them. Change anything that requires alteration to meet their needs.

Vocal variety is very important, as is intonation. For an

audience which has good vision, gestures or visual aids can add substance and interest to a story but, care must be taken to include those people whose vision or hearing may be somewhat challenged.

Once Helen attended a storytelling presentation at which she sat next to a sight-impaired person. Although he couldn't see any of the action he was enthralled by the teller's delivery of the story. He missed none of the action and he noticed many little things in the oral part of the presentation that Helen had failed to perceive.

Pauses work for you

Don't be afraid of silence. Fear of a long pause — of standing, saying nothing in front of an audience — is the mark of an inexperienced performer. Pace your story to keep your audience with you. Pause and give people time to absorb your tale and participate in recreating your vision.

Rest them, after a long period of drama and excitement. Play with them — storytelling should be an enjoyable experience for both audience and teller. When the audience sees you are enjoying yourself, they will relax and join in.

Transfer your vision

Researchers investigating the connection of minds and thoughts, conducted an experiment with an audience, in which two groups of primary school children were told a story. One group was read a story about events which took place in a forest. The other group was told the same story with the teller recalling events as he saw them in his mind's eye — the story unfolding as if on a TV screen inside his head.

Both groups were then asked to draw the trees in the forest as they imagined them to be. The first group, who'd heard the 'read story' drew many different types of trees. The second group, who were 'told' the story, drew firs in the Christmas tree style, just as the teller had visualised them.

Try to clearly visualise your stories so you can pass on your vision to your audience. You'll be a better storyteller if you develop this technique.

Ways of telling

There are as many different ways of telling stories as there are tellers. Some are quiet and subdued, like the Irish Shanahee, who sits comfortably in a chair and just recounts the story, letting the words he weaves carry the magic to his listeners.

Others, like Tennessee teller, Anndrena Belcher, bounce around involving and dragging in the audience, making them participate in her story. Anndrena uses costumes to dress her stories, plays guitar and sings. Then again, she can just stand and reduce her audience to tears with the emotions of her personal stories. Seeing her in action is a chance not to be missed.

Gail Herman, organic storyteller, lets the audience compose the tale with her, as she becomes the orchestra leader. Gail uses musical instruments, many different kinds of puppets and is skilled in mime.

Margaret Read MacDonald, the guru of audience participation stories, uses chants, mime, song and repetitive actions to carry her audience along with her. The audience experiences a sharing of the story in a most enjoyable way.

 Yuri, the Russian Storyteller, begins by lighting the story candle. Once his candle is lit, no-one but the storyteller speaks, unless they are invited to do so. When he is finished, the candle is snuffed out and the audience is in no doubt that the story has ended.

All of these storytellers use different mechanisms to get their audiences involved in their story. Experiment and develop your own style of telling to suit your category of audience. Once you have their attention the audience is yours for the length of your storytelling presentation.

Adult audiences

There is very little difference between child and adult audiences. Both love a well-told story. A good example of stories suitable for both adult and child audiences would be 'The Little Old Lady Who Lived in a Vinegar Bottle'. The theme of constant dissatisfaction is relevant to all stages of human life and we can all identify with its message.

Every adult has a child inside them and we found that a number of the story presentations we offer to children work equally well with adult audiences. We find this especially so with Berice's stories, when she uses her amazing collection of hand and finger puppets. Adult audiences are entranced by the puppets.

Stories with a simple theme are most appropriate for young children. They should generally be of short duration to match the children's shorter attention span. Storytelling for children is often used for educational purposes or to encourage an interest in reading books. In the case of adults, stories are more often told for enjoyment, to make a point or explain a message.

Adult audiences to whom we have presented stories include hard-headed businessmen, Rotary and Lions clubs, women's clubs, shoppers' clubs and Golden Age groups of men and women. They have all enjoyed presentations in which we use and talk about the puppets and other aids, such as Helen's rain-stick.

Adult storytelling allows you to introduce longer, more complex stories, dealing with mature themes. Be careful to select stories which will hold their interest and attention. If possible, create a repertoire of stories with themes that concern adults. Themes such as adventure, crime, sport, history, overcoming adversity, love, hate, anger, family, death, ageing and friendship.

Don't forget to include some interactive stories in your program. Adults really enjoy becoming involved and participating in the stories. We all love to play and these stories allow adults to cast aside their inhibitions for a short while, to join in and share in some fun with the storyteller and each other.

Adding a selection of personal stories to your collection is a good idea. They can be drawn from your own life or the lives of those close to you. Wherever they come from personal stories are always popular with adults, whose range of experience enables them to identify with many of the situations you describe.

Give them the opportunity to go home afterwards and tell their families the stories you have awakened in them by telling your stories.

5 *Story Reading*

STORYTELLING purists preach that stories should be 'told heart to heart'. But it isn't always possible, or practical, for this to take place. While it is more satisfying to 'tell' stories to an audience, don't allow these outdated attitudes to stop you reading stories to your audiences if you haven't the time to learn them.

Librarians, teachers, writers and others (such as working parents) who work to stringent time constraints, may not have the luxury of time to build up a repertoire of stories. So it is important that the act of story reading is practised effectively.
The story must excite and grab the audience's attention but, more importantly, the teller must be enthusiastic, even passionate, about the chosen story.

Be aware that when you read a written version of a story, you have to compensate for losing approximately two-thirds of your storytelling instrument: the unhindered gestures of your body, face and hands; the natural pace; vocal variety and timing. As well, you have to complete all of the pictures for the listeners.

When telling a story, you are more free to tune into the signals you receive from the audience's body language and can more easily infer 'message received' and so continue to the next point.

The story reader whose eyes are at times on the page is less able to receive those silent cues from the audience. Therefore the skills of audience involvement are even more important to the story reader than they are to a storyteller. Strong visual bonding is necessary to enable a connection of minds (engagement) between reader and audience. Only then will you and your audience be likely to create a similar picture from the words you used. Take a little extra time to connect with your audience before you start to read.

Always be aware of what text lies ahead (as the newsreaders are on television) and look up at the audience's faces to establish strong eye contact. You want your listeners to be co-creating mental pictures with you throughout the reading. Changes of pace and the use of pause are also vital in story reading to allow the audience time to interpret the text.

Whilst you can change and update the words — leaving out unnecessary or outdated language — you should also vary the speed at which the story is read, to suit each audience. (The exception to this occurs in more formal, literary readings, in which every word must be read as published).

To help breathe life and colour into the text a dramatic reading depends on vocal variety and good intonation. A flat monotone will only switch off your listeners and they'll become bored and restless.

Where you are able, have several different readers present a portion of the story, so no-one becomes tired. This gives variety to a long piece of prose.

So the audience can join in a chorus, print the words on a board or a card which a child or other helper can hold up for you. An example of this would be the repetitive lines from Wanda Gag's story, 'Millions of Cats':

Cats here, cats there,
Cats and kittens everywhere,
Hundreds of cats, thousands of cats,
Millions and billions and trillions of cats.

Children really love to join in and recite the chorus of this popular old story. Their response to the chorus is as enthusiastic today as when it was first written. Give all your audiences the opportunity to enjoy participating with you in the storytelling. When well executed it gives the teller a great sense of achievement.

Picture books

The picture books of today are pure magic due to the high standard of artwork and improvements in modern inks and printing technology. The exciting use of colour, clear reproduction techniques and innovative artwork enhance the text to entrance the reader.

Many of these books have become collectors' items because of the brilliant illustrations they contain. Try to acquire some of the super-sized picture books now being produced for easy reading.

Picture books come in two types: those accompanied by text and those which have no text at all. The books without text are wonderful mechanisms for developing creative storytelling with a group of children. The pictures may each be interpreted by individual children to create a group story. As children's imaginations are different, no two story sessions will ever be the same.

When offering stories from picture books with text, I usually read the story first. Then I go through the story a second time, showing the pictures. I like my listeners to hear the words and visualise the story in their minds first.

Other story readers show the pictures, holding the book to one side, while reading the text. If you do this, make sure, when you hold up the illustrations, that you can easily read the words accompanying the pictures. Make certain all the children, especially those at the back or sides, can easily see the pictures you show them. *Check with them to be sure.* Choose large, bold, bright picture books that are easily seen, with print styles you can read comfortably.

There is no single way to read stories; experiment and find out which technique works best for you. Do your preparation ahead and practise reading to get your timing and display of the illustrations synchronised. Taking this time to prepare for your story-time session allows you the opportunity to make that connection to your listeners with eye contact and body language.

Readings for children are usually conducted in a room in which the reader is seated in front of a group, which is sitting close together on a mat on the floor. Back up from your audience a little, so the pictures can be easily seen without you having to wave the book around. Find the centre of the group and tell from that position allowing sufficient space in front of you so the children can all see the pictures.

Remember that any pauses or breaks in the story make it more difficult to hold the audience's interest, so it is important to keep the story flowing.

Story selection for readings

For books which are not illustrated, selection is even more important. In this case the reader is trying to encourage the audience to develop a love of reading and a respect for books. Trying to encourage children's reading will demand a good knowledge of the books offered.

The book selection should be exciting and relevant to the interests of the listeners. Choose books which will appeal to your audience's imagination, stories which children like and request, and about which you feel passionate.

Choose books which are topical — perhaps the selection from the Children's Book of the Year listing, or other favourites, such as *Charlotte's Web*, *Sadako and the Thousand Paper Cranes*,

Paul Jennings' stories, or Aboriginal stories, like *The Rainbow Serpent*, and, *Ngalculli the Red Kangaroo*.

The Story of Rosy Dock, a book written and illustrated by Jeanie Baker, could be read to promote discussion about ecology and the damage caused to the environment by introduced plant species.

When reading to older children, offer a selection from a couple of contrasting books which will give them a wider choice. If you are presenting a series of readings, present one book of the selection as a serial in several episodic parts. Read from this book over a number of weeks, finishing with an exciting cliff-hanger each time, to bring the listeners back, eager for further story sessions or to encourage them to borrow the book for themselves.

Be aware of the attention span of your audience and offer a selection of stories which allow for some type of audience involvement. Encourage the participants to take part somewhere in the storytime. There are many stories which involve rhythmic movement: clapping, finger clicking and gestures. Search for opportunities to use these as part of your telling. Have the children act out the story; it's amazing how creative they can be.

Audiences should be divided into suitable age groups so each story can be tailored to the attention span, vocabulary level, and interests of the group. To increase your chance of success, don't attempt to span too wide a spread of ages. Children's audiences should not include more than four consecutive grade levels and must always include parent-helpers or teachers to keep order. If you are reading to a large group, you are too busy presenting the story to have to monitor unruly children's behaviour.

Aim to offer successful story readings and enjoyable experiences. If possible, try to find time to learn some stories and re-tell these often. Build yourself a small but expanding repertoire, which is available at short notice. Some of these should include the interactive stories which can help break the discomfort of sitting still for a long time.

Margaret Read MacDonald's *Twenty Tellable Tales* and *The Storyteller's Start-up Book* contain a number of interactive stories ready for immediate use. (See Bibliography)

6   *Interactive Storytelling*

A UDIENCE participation stories are special, both for teller and audience. They are a form of 'group play'. A really enthusiastic audience can sweep teller and story along with its excitement. You can use hand clapping, or finger clicking, foot stamping, songs, chants, or musical instruments to involve your audience.

When telling a story with repetitive lines in it, you will notice audience members mouthing or repeating the words along with you. Encourage them to join in with a wave of the hand or an invitation to 'come along and help me'. In this way your story becomes a mutual creation.

To enable your audience to participate in your story, pause at times and ask them to help with the name or event you are about to describe. Build responses into your stories wherever appropri-

ate. By telling them the responses and practising with them, prior to starting your story, it is easier to set the scene. If your audience starts to join in spontaneously, keep the fun going and go with the flow.

Be careful not to let the audience get out of control and take over your story.

31

Before you put your foot on the accelerator, be sure you know how to engage the brake.

Make sure you have worked out a mechanism for controlling the interaction. Helen uses a rain-stick to excellent effect. Its soft swishing sound quickly calms an over-exuberant audience and places her back in control. Simple hand gestures are equally effective.

Taking part in stories builds confidence in timid youngsters. They like to feel that they are part of the performance without actually having to stand in front of the group. If they are shy at first, don't worry about it. They will soon warm up as the program continues and energy builds.

If you find your audience is reluctant to participate in your story, don't panic. Just continue telling the story and, with a smile and a wave of the hands in the participation spots, encourage them to join you.

If they are still reluctant, you've lost nothing, just carry on with the story. Remember, to make it easier for them to join in, it can help to have a flip-chart or a copy of the words on the board.

No two audiences are exactly alike. Sometimes you may appear to be getting little audible response. (This is particularly so with Asian audiences.) Be flexible and enjoy the game — you could be quite surprised after the telling, to hear how much a 'reserved' audience actually enjoyed themselves.

Don't forget to thank an audience for their participation in your story. You are guaranteed a greater response next time if the audience feels you appreciate their efforts. Storytelling is truly a sharing experience.

Plan ahead

Problems can arise at the other end of the participation scale, where an audience becomes too exuberant. If your story calls for a loud chorus of sound, remember to arrange, ahead of time, for a signal to turn it off. Failure to do this can pose problems for some less assertive tellers.

Plan your program so you can bring the audience back to reality with a quieter story to finish the session. A teacher does not appreciate having a class handed back all hyped up and ready to swing from the chandeliers.

Audience participation is not limited to merely joining in with words and chants. Members of the audience can assist with the telling. The teller may engage an audience member by pretending he is a story character and asking a question directly. Audience members can also assist with props, mime or dance within the story space.

Helen tells a story in which several children from the audience participate by taking parts in the performance, while the audience is asked to join in with a chorus of sounds. It is a favourite tale and everyone has lots of fun and that's what storytelling is about.

Stories can be told without recourse to the spoken word. They can be conveyed as well in art, music, dance and mime. New Zealand tellers, Apirana and Rangimoana Taylor, tell their stories twice — once in words and, again silently with incredibly beautiful and moving dance or mime — leaving the audience to interpret the movement.

Although it is not appropriate to participate in all stories, if you try to build some audience responses into your own story writing, wherever possible, it will allow that essential connection with the audience.

You will usually find your audience enjoys the 'participation stories' more than the ones where they are passive and simply listen. Plan your programs carefully so you achieve a balance between the active and passive stories.

Be creative, whatever your style of telling, get the audience involved.

7 *Organic Storytelling*

I N organic storytelling the teller asks the audience for help in composing the story. The teller is really the 'conductor' of the performance, calling up the next response from the audience or 'orchestra' — unsure of what it will be until it is given. She has to be able to adjust the next section of her story to the evolving circumstances.

Here is an organic story which we have devised as an example of the form. The *_____ indicates where audience input is required.

*_____(title to be decided at the conclusion of the story)
Once upon a time there was a good little boy/girl *_____ named *_____ who lived near a beach in the suburb of *_____. Everyone knew how good *_____ was. All the neighbourhood children became tired of continually hearing from their parents about how *_____ always tidied up his/her *_____ and cleaned *_____, and helped with *_____ and ate all *_____ and *_____. *_____ never forgot to feed his/her pet *_____ and clean its *_____.

One day all the children gathered together to tell *_____ how his/her reputation for exceptionally good behaviour was bugging them. At this meeting they decided to invite *_____ to a *_____. *_____ was really quite a nice person and fun to be around and the others were sure they could work out a plan to *_____ his/her *_____. When *_____ arrived at the *_____ he/she was surprised at what the others had to say.

He/she thought that all children *_____ and *_____ for their parents. He/she was an orphan, and lived with his/her *_____ who were much older than the other children's parents. If *_____ didn't do the tasks set for him/her by his/her *_____ she/he might have to go to *_____.

Hearing this the other children felt *_____ and *_____ for her/him. They decided not to become *_____ whenever their parents said how good *_____ was. They'd just *_____. Everyone wanted to be *_____'s friend after that.

Gail Herman is the master of this sort of situation, and her delighted shriek of 'You're right!' brings a beaming smile, as the youngsters direct the course of the tale. This builds a sense of achievement for children who may not have 'got anything right' all week. Often they will tell you how much they enjoyed being part of your story.

Gail says, 'Never reject any idea volunteered. Take it and link it into the next event.' To spark ideas, she frequently asks her listeners, 'What do you think happened next?' Gail may invite the audience to close their eyes and imagine the action, and to raise their hands when they are ready to share it.

This style of storytelling is not an easy method if you are a novice teller; all too often you could find yourself 'painted into a corner', with nowhere to turn for your story's conclusion. Perhaps some blue-eyed moppet with the face of an angel may elect to chop off your hero's head in the first minute of your tale.

Therefore you must be flexible and prepared to redirect the course of the story when it looks as though it's becoming irretrievably cornered.

Research some of the traditional stories such as 'Stone Soup',

'The Enormous Turnip', 'The Three Billy Goats Gruff', and adapt them so your audience has the opportunity to change some

of the action. This will give them the freedom to bring today's language and values into the story, making it interesting and fun.

Reduce the story to its bare bones: characters, setting, object, problems and resolution. Change one or more of these elements to link the story with a new idea, such as Christmas, or camping, or some other special occasion.

Maybe the story could remain intact in all but the time setting. Make it happen in a future time.

Try some of these ideas and you may find yourself creating some wonderful new story opportunities. The spontaneity of the style can elicit unusual and original responses into an otherwise stale or old-fashioned style of storytelling.

I can guarantee your audience will enjoy their involvement. Everyone loves to participate in a fun-filled performance.

Don't forget to bring them back!

Don't leave your audience in limbo back there in storyland. After one of these vigorous performances, cool off, or slow down, the audience with a more quietly paced story or poem, before you bring them back to the reality of 'here and now'.

If you opened your performance with music or some other type of ritual, close it in a similar fashion to bring them quietly in to reality. Making that connection back is a most important part of your storytelling.

8 Personal Stories

EVERYONE is a storyteller. We all have stories to tell. Although stories of peoples' lives seem clearer when viewed as a whole, we don't need to wait that long given all the predicaments, nonsense, joys and surprises that life deals out to us. The stories of what happened along the way are just as fascinating.

Stories don't have to be folk tales, fairytales or heroic legends. But you can use these mythical tales as a structure on which to hang your personal stories, linking them together creatively.

The greatest source of story material comes from our own lives, our experiences, and those of our families. Analyse what the purpose is in telling your personal stories and develop a great repertoire of real-life stories you have tailored for telling.

Every person, every culture, has a wealth of stories to tell. Capturing and using these stories weaves the complex fabric of everyone's common experiences to expose the universal truths and wisdom they contain. Sharing each other's personal stories is a great way to bridge community and age differences.

Often these stories are more descriptive or reflective of a society which existed at the time we grew up. They are humorous local character sketches of family members and the community around us.

Tell your personal stories so that people can identify with them. You want your audiences to relate your stories to their lives, so that when they go home they will tell their families the stories you have kindled in their memories.

Personal stories have the most impact. After all, you know everything about those experiences. You have available all the emotions and feelings surrounding the actions you are recounting. In telling personal stories, you are not just dealing with words and hearsay. This is real-life stuff.

Use some family characters

For instance, every family has an eccentric member, somewhere. Old Uncle Fred, who has done memorable things while, perhaps, a little 'under the weather'; or Aunt Maude, with a heart of gold, who 'didn't suffer fools gladly'. Her brushes with neighbours and tradespeople have become family legends. Now ageing rapidly, her reality is changing, with memories floating between the past and the present. Such a character as Aunt Maude allows for great stories.

Places where you've lived make good stories. They are the settings for the stories of major or memorable events in your life.

Bygone days provide stories: about the problems encountered getting water from a well, or going to the dunny out the back, especially the long drop variety, where spiders, snakes, and stark terror lurked. Tell stories about what it was like growing up during the great depression, or wartime, with its rationing of

necessities. Tell of how we 'made do'. Maybe you can tell stories of drought experiences and how the traumas they brought altered the direction of your life and those of your family. Later generations may never experience any of these hardships, so your stories will bring understanding.

Stories of how the direction of your life and work changed due to the invention of modern equipment (such as, the computer or microwave oven) will provide lessons in life and make your audience think about flexibility and adaptability and life's contrasts.

Tell your personal stories whenever you can and you'll find people will stop what they're doing and listen, fascinated by your experiences. Your stories are unique to your life and although others may have experienced similar occurrences the details and the impact on their life is never the same. Keep telling these stories to help build up the dynamics of your storytelling art.

Children love to hear stories about what it was like when their parents and grandparents were young. Times have changed very rapidly with the advancement of knowledge and development of technology. Conditions which existed in your youth are very difficult to imagine today.

Childhood, of course, provides a great fund of stories from which to draw — ask any grandparent. Grandchildren love hearing stories about when they were tiny. Whenever there is a family get-together, you will receive many requests to repeat their favourite stories.

Don't say your family hasn't anything worth telling. Most of us love to peep into events in other peoples' lives. We are fascinated by both the ordinary, everyday events and the extraordinary, one-off occurrences. Once you start delving into your family life, masses of memories and stories worth telling will come tumbling out.

Stories reveal insights

Recalling personal stories engages our feelings and often reveals inner meanings, hidden from us at the time they happened. These stories born of the teller's own unique life experiences, are many-layered, with insights for both the listener and the teller.

The most vivid stories often deal with one or another of life's crises or turning points in which a character faces some form of adversity and overcomes it. The story evolves from the way in which your character deals with the situation and these tales can engender much humour.

Instances of moving and personal stories are:

- *Personal Stories of the American Civil War*, read from original letters by James I. Robertson Jr., Professor of History at the University at Blacksburg, Virginia.
- by Syd Lieberman, *Intrepid Birdmen: Fighter Pilots of World War I*, is written from letters sent home by the young pilots in both wars.
- *The Pink Triangle* — a child's story of survival in Auschwitz as told by the child, Kitty Fischer.
- *Lousy little sixpence*, the story of how Aboriginal children were taken from their mothers to Anglicise them, is by Pamela Vernon, a white orphan girl living in the home to which they were sent.

When listening to a personal story, it is amazing how our memories and emotions of similar experiences can be unexpectedly recalled. Once this connection or link to our own life is made we are more easily moved, sometimes to tears.

Patti Miller, a writer and teacher of autobiography, has this to say in her latest book, *Writing Your Life*, (Allen & Unwin, 1994):

> Everyone can write a life story. If you have dreamed by childhood creeks, played in a dusty school yard, watcheds the sunrise after a partner has died, or lived through any of life's twists and turns, then you have a story to tell.

It is challenging to examine your life but it can also be rewarding. As you select stories to tell, you grow in understanding and self-knowledge. Reviewing events that happened in your childhood can offer new insights, when you examine them with adult understanding.

For example, while attending a Storytellers' Festival in New Zealand, we listened to Syd Lieberman tell stories about his children. We laughed till our sides were sore and our merriment was increased as the stories he recounted reminded us of incidents and experiences in our own families.

A short while later he told his *Intrepid Birdmen – The Fighter Pilots of World War I* story — powerful stuff! I was moved but Helen was overwhelmed by emotion and tears. Suddenly, she had gained insight into her father's harrowing World War I experiences, when as barely more than a youth he'd fought in Europe in 1914–1918. Insights into the indescribable horrors of a war fought in the mud and trenches of Passchendaele, involving such awful weapons as mustard gas. Fighting in that war had entirely changed his former easy-going, likeable personality into the harsh disciplinarian she knew and grew to hate as a child. Syd's storytelling brought Helen understanding — even bestowed forgiveness — for her father's moods and violent behaviour. Yes, story does have the power to heal old wounds!

Stories reveal courage

Family stories, the setting down of trials and achievements and the silent heroism of 'ordinary people', can reveal unrecognised strength and courage.

Recently, when conducting a Speechcraft course we came across an example of this courage. There were four women who'd joined the class to improve their speaking skills, so that they could successfully lobby politicians. Each has a severely handicapped child, fast approaching adulthood, and the stories of their everyday lives are truly heroic. They care for these adult children, year in and year out. Their stories are true epic tales of love, despair and humour. During the telling of their stories the women were frequently overcome with emotions, which were shared by those present. This sharing of emotions, when people are on the one wavelength, is what storytelling is all about. As Patti Miller, points out in *Writing Your Life*:

> A rare trust and warmth are generated when you offer the story of your life to another. There is wonder in the difference of our lives and, at the same time, joy in knowing that we are so much alike.

Anndrena Belcher, a hillbilly storyteller from Tennessee, whom we first met last year at Masterton, New Zealand, at the Glistening Waters International Festival, tells wonderful stories of her early years, growing up in the mountains of Tennessee. She tells stories about her Grammaw Mimmo, who played a large part in her life.

Anndrena has the ability to take her audience from laughter to tears and back again very quickly. As we shared the emotions of the events in her Grammaw's life and related them to events in ours, Berice sat there with tears dripping off her chin, hoping no-one was looking in her direction.

Recently we experienced a program of storytelling called, 'Sometimes we need a story more than food', presented by Corey Fischer, who was visiting from San Francisco. Some of his stories were of personal experiences intermingled with mythical tales and we sat in awe of his creative talent. Among the stories he shared were very personal ones of his relationship with his parents, his father in particular.

We all identified with the story of when he was lost in Los Angeles as an eight-year-old child. There are many times in our lives when we become lost; Corey showed us we all share similar experiences. We also enjoyed his subtle humour in the tales he shared of his experiences in trying to bridge the gap over the years between his father (who later suffered from Alzheimer's) and himself. I'm sure the audience left with many of their own life memories rekindled — part of the work of a good storyteller.

Personal stories are a most powerful teaching tool. Anyone who has read Dale Carnegie's best-selling book, *How to Win Friends and Influence People*, will remember his format. National Speakers' workshop presenters suggest that to reinforce the point you are making:

- tell a personal story to illustrate it. If you haven't a personal story,
- adapt someone else's, or
- link to it, by claiming it happened to a relative or friend of yours.

How do you find a personal story?

When developing a personal story the following points are worth considering:

- To whom are you telling the story?
- What point do you want to make?
- How did the central event in the story begin?
- Where did the action occur?
- When did it occur?
- Who was involved?
- What were the chief characters like?
- What made you remember it?
- What happened?
- How was it resolved?
- What does the story say about you?
- How does it relate to the point you are making?

Ideas for personal stories

Some suggestions for personal stories (stories from your childhood or daily life) are as follows:

- Something unforgettable you did at home, school, or work which caused you problems.
- An exciting game or contest you played and won — or lost.
- An unforgettable camping trip, holiday or bush walk.
- An experience with flood, fire, storm or an accident.
- A nightmare or dream.
- An unforgettable family member: hero, rascal, villain.

- Something unforgettable your pet did — good or bad.
- Did you ever lose something special? Was it ever found? How?
- A Pyrrhic victory: an argument you won, but, in the end, felt you'd lost.
- An idea that really worked for you.
- How you played a joke on someone and how it back-fired.
- Your most embarrassing moments — we all have them.
- Your worst travel experience.
- Your funniest holiday experience.

From the short list I've given, you can see that stories can come from any angle. Simple everyday stories can become intriguing for a stranger who doesn't know much about you.

Why not try to write down some stories which these suggestions have triggered in your memory — you may find some good story material there.

Mine your life experiences for the hidden treasures; you will discover gems just waiting to be polished and set in a story. There is pleasure in telling and reliving past events.

9 *The Tools of Storytelling*

S TORYTELLERS have only three basic tools to work with: words, their voice and body. It is important that each of these components works effectively to create the best impression possible.

Words

The Power of Words

Soft words will put a babe to sleep. Excited words will stir a mob to violence. Eloquent words will send armies marching into the face of death. Encouraging words will fan to flame the genius of a Rembrandt or a Lincoln. Powerful words will mould the public mind as the sculptor moulds his clay. Words are a dynamic force.

Words are the swords we use in our battle for success and happiness. How others react towards us depends, in a large measure, upon the words we speak to them. Life is a great whispering gallery that sends back echoes of the words we send out! Our words are immortal, too. They go marching through the years in the lives of all those with whom we come in contact. When you speak, when you write, remember the creative power of words.

—Wilfred A. Peterson. From *Jokes, Quotes and One-Liners for Public Speakers* by Henry V. Prochnow and Henry V. Prochnow Jr., Thorsons, 1983.

If all we have to work with are words, we must make sure that we have mastery over a comprehensive collection of these wonderful tools. We are lucky that the English language, one of the richest, is our native tongue. English has absorbed (and adopted) words from almost every other language. Most people have a larger reading than oral vocabulary, made up of words we have read, but never actually pronounced or used in conversation. According to Dr Wilfred Funk, who wrote 'It Pays to Increase Your Word Power' for a popular magazine, 'The average person has a spoken vocabulary of about 200 words, which he uses all the time and recognises only about another 2000 words'.

The Macquarie Dictionary contains 2000 *new* words (neologisms) which have been added to our language in the last ten years. When we realise that new words are continually being added to the language, we need to actively work at learning these new additions just to keep up with the changes.

That doesn't take into account the words which have changed their meanings over the years. There are many words in current use which have quite different meanings from what they did when we were young. For instance, when we were young, 'gay' meant lively, merry, or cheerful; today it refers to homosexuals. 'Grass' back then was for mowing and 'pot' was for cooking in. Today, they refer to marijuana. Then there are acronyms such as 'yuppie', derived from the first letters of 'young, urban, professional person'.

When we look at the way the language is changing, evolving if you like, we can see how easily we could be left behind if we don't make a conscious effort to keep abreast of the changes. Regardless of how good our present vocabulary is, there is value in increasing it.

If we are going to work with words which convey our images we want the very best selection from which to choose. We want those words which will convey precise shades of meaning.

If you were an artist you wouldn't attempt to paint a picture without a full palette of colours. You wouldn't make do with a brown instead of a blue shading for a mountain lake or sky. To get the exact colour needed to reproduce your vision on to the canvas, you'd mix and blend until you had achieved the correct shade.

As a storyteller you need to find the exact word to paint your imaginary pictures — the very best word available in your linguistic paintbox.

Therefore, in order to weave magic and music with words, you have to be familiar with, and appreciative of, a large and varied vocabulary. The more comprehensive the collection of old friends you have in your vocabulary, the less likely you are to fumble and hesitate while searching for the right word or phrase.

What is a word?

'A word is any single symbol used in speech or writing.' What a deceptively simple definition that is! It's correct, of course, but makes no mention of the power of words which have changed the course of history. Examples of some simple, inspirational, but powerful words used in written or spoken forms are as follows:

'I have a dream that one day this nation will rise up and live out the true meaning of its creed: We hold these truths to be self-evident; that all men are created equal.' — from a speech by Martin Luther King Jr.

'When we let freedom ring . . . all of God's children will be able to join hands and sing in the words of the old Negro spiritual, Free at last! Free at last! Thank God Almighty, we are free at last!' — from a speech by Martin Luther King Jr.

'We shall fight them on the beaches' — from a speech by Winston Churchill during World War II.

Or those truly simple words which have caused tremendous joy and problems for millions of people. 'I love you', 'I do', and 'Charge it!'

How do we use words?

Words are only symbols. Symbols that can be used to manipulate the minds of our audiences.

The best speakers, storytellers and advertising people target their audiences precisely. They research what the words they use mean to the particular audience to whom their message is directed, carefully planning their stories and texts so as to meet on the same wavelength as their audience. This ensures success. As David Ogilvy, guru of advertising, says in *Ogilvy on Advertising* (1983): 'Copy should be written in the language people use in everyday conversation.'

Do your research as he did. Find out all you can about your audience's idiosyncrasies and tailor your words to meet their needs. This will allow you to make a better connection with them when telling your stories.

Berice has always been enthusiastic about words. She says:

As a ten-year old I read my dictionary from cover to cover, priding myself on an extensive vocabulary. My favourite words were 'sludge', 'mellifluous', 'Mississippi' and 'onomatopoeia'.

When seeking out a picture book a few weeks ago, for a storytelling session with three-year-olds, I came across a book with a whole series of words I had never seen before. I couldn't believe they were real, so I checked in the encyclopaedia on animal group terminology. What I found there, was over a hundred examples of these words, which I had never known.

Did you know that a collection of finches is called a charm? A group of magpies, a tiding? A collection of nightingales, a watch? And a group of turkeys is called a rafter? (It might make you feel better to know that even the salespeople at the local turkey processing plant didn't know that one).

All this came as a blow to my pride and set me looking around the dictionary shelf at the local library. I found two books: *The Wit's Dictionary*, which I would recommend to all speakers, writers and storytellers, and the wonderfully fun *Dictionary of Ridiculous Words*.

Look around the bookshops and libraries for books which will help increase your word power. Spend some spare time developing a wider vocabulary. Knowing precisely the right word to use when telling your stories pays dividends. Like the artist's palette of colours, a selection of words from a comprehensive vocabulary helps to convey your vision of the story to the minds of your audience.

The Voice

The storyteller's performance instrument is the voice. Therefore it is important that you respect and care for your voice in the same way you would for an antique Stradivarius violin.

Exercises for the Voice

Develop correct deep-breathing through exercises which you should practise daily to strengthen your vocal output and relax your body and mind. Ten minutes of these breathing exercises each day will soon result in greater control of your breath and voice. Find a spot outside and enthusiastically practise these routines, preferably where the air is bracing.

Breathe from your abdomen. Practise completely emptying your lungs and, with each new breath, expand your lungs to maximum capacity. Place your hands on your abdomen, to check that you are breathing correctly. Lie on a mat on the ground and breathe deeply from the abdomen. Repeat the action ten times. Now stand up. Try it again ten times standing up.

When speaking, you don't need to fill your lungs to maximum capacity. Your body knows automatically how much air you need.

To eliminate the necessity for using 'he said, she said', and such like, increase your awareness of the many ways in which you can use your voice to highlight the differences between the characters in your stories.

Begin by using your voice in the 'head area' which produces a very high, wiry, nasal sound. Recite a poem or a few lines to hold the tone up there.

Next, move your voice down to your chest area and, again,

practise for several minutes. The chest gives a lower, more pleasant tone. This is a good sound for narration.

Drop your voice to your abdomen level for an even lower, fuller sound. Practise speaking some lines to hold the tone in your belly.

Finally, lower your voice so it seems to come from your boots. This voice is very deep and resonant — suitable for the 'giant', 'baddie' or 'authority figure' in fairy stories.

Before you start each day, spend some time practising the range of vowel sounds, as well as 's' sounds to eliminate sibilant, or lisping 's' sounds. You can do these in the bathroom, as you take your morning bath or shower. Use your tape-recorder to identify problems.

The acoustics of this confined space will assist you and having a mirror to work with is also a help. To help you articulate correctly work with the 'r' sounds and word endings such as 'ing', 'ed', 'ck', 'es', 't', 'p', and so on. Practise the 'mmm-nnn' buzzing sounds and the 'eeee-oooo-aaaa' sounds.

If you are trying to develop dialects practise moving the sound around, backwards and forwards in your mouth. The dialects will come with experimentation and practise and close listening to clear examples.

Allow at least half an hour each day, if you can manage it, to practise these voice exercises and improve your articulation.

When driving the car on the way to a telling, practise your piece, or sing along with the radio to widen the range of tone and pitch in your voice. Helen often does this and receives some strange looks when she's stopped at traffic lights. You'll be surprised how much this simple exercise will help to add colour to your performance (and, possibly, your social life).

Maintain hydration

Water is excellent for the brain. To maintain hydration, drink plenty of water prior to your performance — at least two litres per day and three to four litres on the day before. This will prevent your body becoming dehydrated and will help improve your memory. In 1994 a leading Canadian psychiatrist advised that, 'Failure to drink enough water leads to poor memory, lack of concentration and perhaps, plays a part in the onset of senility and dementia.'

On the day of your performance make sure you start out by drinking at least one litre of water. Avoid drinking coffee and tea or other stimulants prior to and during your performance; they affect your memory and, it is suggested, adversely affect your voice. A tumbler of warmish water to sip will help if you are having problems with a dry mouth or throat.

Body language

When you are addressing an audience, your body sends two types of messages — verbal and non-verbal. This latter yields a great deal of information about how you feel, mentally and physically.

If you are nervous, your body tightens up and transmits your fear to the audience. Fear causes your facial expression and body gestures to become tight and frozen. Consequently, your audience reflects that expression. Could this be the reason why some audiences don't respond as you would wish?

I once watched a performance where a teller was suffering from a severe dose of stage fright. Her miserable demeanour transferred directly to her listeners who adopted her feelings of tension and misery. Only when she relaxed and smiled did they respond with warmth. Once they felt she was enjoying the experience, the audience allowed itself to do the same.

If you adopt a positive approach and develop a more relaxed style of presenting, there is a greater chance of your audience being relaxed. This way they'll be better prepared to enjoy your performance.

Breathe deeply at pauses, smile often and relax. Your audience will respond in kind, warming to your obviously comfortable expression and relaxed behaviour. Remember they want to like you and enjoy your presentation.

Your body conveys information through your eye contact and expression, your body, hand and facial gestures, so it is important that you make these features work for you.

Don't just stand still like a dummy in a shop window. Move! People lose interest in still life — things that don't move. This doesn't mean you should flap your hands about like a bird with trimmed wings trying to fly. Use your hand gestures where they are most effective. When making a gesture with your hand, extend your whole hand and forearm outwards, so the audience sees you mean business.

Develop your gestures by watching yourself performing in a mirror. Discard any distracting mannerisms, such as hand-flapping, rocking, swaying and pacing. Stop fiddling with your pockets, pimples, hair, jewellery, or belt and let your hands drop into a comfortable position so you can concentrate on the story you are telling. If necessary, to keep your hands from waving about, hold an item such as a candle, rain-stick or puppet. You can use any of these to add drama to your story.

Assume a comfortable posture to help you breathe and speak more easily. Let your shoulders relax and your hands hang loosely but comfortably at your sides, with your fingers slightly drawn together. (Don't use the fig leaf position.)

How can gestures help your presentation?

Body gestures are important because they are a natural visual aid to support your words. When used effectively they can dissipate your nervous energy, lending drama and emphasis to your words. Some gestures can help develop audience participation in your stories. But ensure that your gestures do not distract the audience.

Helen often uses gestures to invite the audience to join in repetitive choruses with her—gestures which are introduced to the audience before beginning the story. She also uses different gestures to slow down or cut off audience participation when she wishes to continue telling her story.

When using hand gestures in a large room make sure the people at the back can see you clearly (this is important if you are short). You may need to use a stage or podium to add height or, if none is available, use gestures from shoulder height.

Practise making these exaggerated gestures so that you become comfortable with these movements before doing them in front of an audience. Always consider your audience, making sure they all get to see and hear your performance equally.

Transitions and movement

When telling a story in which there are a number of transitions — changes from high-intensity drama to low-intensity drama — try to use movement to emphasise and dramatise that transition.

While the audience is briefly resting during one of these transitions, Helen moves in a triangular direction from the *high ground*, ('H', seated right on a higher stool and targeting the left-hand side of the audience) to the *middle ground* ('M',

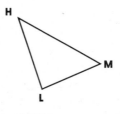

A U D I E N C E

standing forward, three paces towards centre stage, targeting the middle and back audience) and then, at the next transition, to the *low ground* ('L', left two paces side-back, seated on a lower stool, targeting the right hand side of the audience).

The whole movement area resembles an uneven triangle. She uses a low stool for the 'low ground' and a higher bar stool for the 'high ground' (see diagram). Helen stands when in the 'middle ground'.

Try this at home until you become comfortable enough to put it into practise. Don't attempt to speak during the transitions; you'll lose your audience.

Remember: Move — speak. Move — speak.

It takes quite some practice to develop a smooth transition style but it is worth the effort. Maintain eye contact with the whole audience but keep it more focussed on the targeted area.

At times people in her audiences have commented that they have felt more closely bonded due to the way in which Helen presented the story.

Because Helen moves around the stage or performance space, she can use those movements to anchor parts of the story. This helps her to remember more clearly where she is in the story.

Work at developing a presentation style to suit your style of telling. *There is no one correct way. Whatever works best for you is the right way.*

Develop eye contact that visually bonds you to your audience and work on those body gestures to build drama and give a greater impact to your presentation.

By developing a comfortable presentation style, through experimentation and lots of practice, you can make storytelling enjoyable for you and your audience.

Develop your word power, voice range and body gestures to enhance your performance and satisfy your audience.

10 Props, Costumes and Other Storytelling Aids

I<small>N</small> earlier times traditional tellers avoided using props. They just stood or sat and told the story. For the children of today's technological age, whose attention span is geared to the five-minute grabs of television, the use of props and aids assists the teller to retain their interest. These may be items such as costumes, musical instruments and puppets, story candles or magic story carpets.

Although props are not essential to storytelling, they are a useful variation, adding flavour to a program in much the same way that you add spice to a recipe. A little adds flavour; too much is overpowering and spoils the effect.

Be aware, though, that any puppet, costume or other device you use will take precedence over the story with an audience, so try to keep their use to a minimum. *Visuals always dominate the verbal content in storytelling.*

Clown, witch, pirate or animal costumes can be used to good effect to create an atmosphere. Merely wearing a 'storytelling outfit' makes you feel special and different from the everyday person you are, when you're not performing. Hats, cloaks, masks and aprons add an extra element of magic to your storytelling. If you come from another culture tell your stories in your national dress.

Amongst our storytellers group we have Romani storytellers, who present their material in national dress from the steps of their gypsy vardo (caravan). They use their dramatic, colourful and rarely seen cultural background to draw a good crowd for their performances.

One of our Sydney tellers, who performs for seniors, has a wonderful presentation in which she uses hats and an instant change of costume — thanks to the magic of velcro — to tell of events from the late 1800s through to the present day.

Her audiences love these props and at some performances, someone comes up with a treasured old hat from their past, to add to her collection. Each of her hats is named for the donor and is acknowledged in her act. She uses each hat as a mnemonic device, or memory trigger, to help with her performance.

Using puppets

Some tellers use puppets — marionettes, hand or finger puppets — which children and many adult audiences love. They are a useful prop for beginners and greatly assist in overcoming self-consciousness.

 Use your puppet to make a point, or act out some dialogue. Then put it out of sight until you next need it. In this way you will keep your audience's attention. If you aim to achieve a smooth presentation the use of puppets needs plenty of practice.

Take some lessons in using puppets and developing voices and dialects from your local Puppetry Guild. The more professional you become in your storytelling, the more you will satisfy your audience and the demand for your services will be greater.

Recently, we worked with a group of Aboriginal children, normally shy and self-conscious in the presence of strangers. With one of Berice's puppets on their hand, each child told their own wonderful story, without any sign of the expected shyness. It was a most enlightening experience for us.

In some of our children's workshops we encourage each child to tell stories using finger puppets. We ask them to concentrate on the puppet on their finger and tell us the story it tells them. This exercise has resulted in some wonderfully creative stories — especially from the very shy children who felt they couldn't possibly tell a story.

If you suffer from stage fright, a storytelling aid such as this could help combat your terror. Also changing into a 'storytelling costume' helps the teller assume a new role and become more focussed on the audience. With a puppet or other aid, such as a rain-stick, to capture the audience's attention, the teller becomes less self-conscious and can become more relaxed.

Remember to keep the height of your puppets constant. *Puppets don't grow taller or shorter during a performance unless the story says so.*

Before you begin to tell the story make sure that the people at the back of the room can see you clearly. If they cannot, change your position so they can more easily see you. Walk up the aisle and take your puppet into the audience if they are having difficulty.

Puppets can be bought through our storytellers' group, or at small specialist shops. Many well-known brands of dressmaking pattern books carry a wide variety of puppet patterns (see *Resources for Storytelling*). Simply sewn, they can inexpensively add spice to your telling. Helen makes all her own hand and finger puppets, which she uses to show children how to tell stories.

Watch your local department or toy stores for bargains in stuffed toys. By undoing seams and removing some of the filling, delightful soft toys can be transformed into hand puppets. A simple inner lining can then be added to hold the puppet's innards together.

It creates quite some amusement in the toy departments of

stores to see me investigating the bottoms of soft toys, looking for potential hand puppets. Parents restrain their children, while shop assistants warily keep an eye on the kinky lady in the toy department.

Be resourceful and creative in acquiring your storytelling aids; they needn't be expensive.

Musical instruments

Musical instruments, especially drums, used to accompany chants and songs are a traditional part of storytelling. In some African countries they are considered an essential part of the story. Creatively add music or sound to your presentations. Music can add a wonderful extra dimension to enrich your stories.

Any music store catalogue lists an assortment of percussion instruments, drums, bells, blocks and gongs. Look around to find a creative way of introducing some of these unusual sounds into your story.

A word of caution. Always check out cultural traditions before purchasing an exotic instrument. Try not to offend your audience. In some cultures, such as the Australian Aboriginal culture, there are certain taboos placed on the handling of their instruments. Women should never handle, or play, the didgeridoo, which is considered to host a male spirit and is a symbol of masculinity.

When storytelling to a group of Aboriginal men recently, Helen noticed an angry reaction from them as she was holding her rain-stick, which looks similar to a didgeridoo. They stood in a group, muttering to each other, with nostrils flaring, sending her negative messages in body language.

Puzzled by their unexpected reaction, she sought a reason for their behaviour. Some moments before the performance was due to commence the penny suddenly dropped: they thought her rain-stick was a didgeridoo. Quickly, she showed them what she held and dispelled their irritation. Fortunately they were fascinated by the rain-stick's soft swishing and trickling sounds. Could it become the next instrument used in their performances?

Instruments from other countries can be used to intrigue and entertain, adding authenticity to regional folk tales. But they don't need to be expensive items. Try to match up your music to the story you are telling. For instance, if you play the banjo, Diane Wolkstein's 'The Banza' story would be a good tale to tell.

Community Aid Abroad shops usually stock a good selection of primitive folk instruments. We have used some of these unusual instruments very successfully, especially when telling to sight-impaired audiences.

Helen's rain stick makes a soft ocean-like sound, which is invaluable in quietening a rowdy audience, and for setting the scene, prior to the 'Once upon a time . . .'. It can be used to make scary night sounds too. Helen likes to use the rippling notes of a South American sitar to transport her audience from 'here and now', to the 'then and there' of her stories.

Gail Herman, the organic storyteller from USA, has a wonderful collection of instruments which she uses to involve her audiences. They include:

- various percussion instruments, such as drums (bongo, hand, and log), tambourines, wood blocks, clapping sticks, temple blocks, and rhythm sticks, maracas, gourds, gongs and finger cymbals;
- thumb piano, xylophone, slide whistle and flexitone;
- kokoriko (Gail's favourite), a small Japanese instrument which is visually engaging, made of slats connected with rope and providing excellent sound effects.

Guitars, woodwind instruments (flutes, pan flutes and tin whistles), harps, didgeridoos and even voices can provide evocative sound effects. The gentle tones of a violin is the perfect accompaniment for some traditional Jewish stories. We used a harp to accompany Diane Wolkstein's performance of 'Psyche and Eros', thus reinforcing the ethereal quality of the myth.

Among many other well-known and unforgettable storytellers I have heard, Mona Williams, originally from Guyana, but now a resident of New Zealand, uses her magnificent singing voice to excellent effect to round out her stories.

Music can add an extra dimension to your performance and you don't need to be a professional musician to include a little music into your telling. Be creative when you shop around for the instrument or other storytelling aid best suited to your style and story.

Remember to practise your chosen instrument though!

11 Story as Therapy

STORYTELLING is a valuable device when utilised in therapy. But be aware that this is a field for specially trained counsellors and specialist psychologists. *If you haven't acquired these qualifications, don't attempt to work in this field without specialist guidance. Untrained people can do much harm.*

In the sophisticated increasingly mobile and techologically oriented world in which we live, we have less time to build and maintain personal relationships. Storytelling has become a valuable means of communication to help bridge personal gaps. People need to talk to other people, especially if they are intensively using electronic equipment during the working week. Storytelling with its personal communication qualities endows that lost sense of connection to another person.

Stories heal

In the past many of the old stories were not used as entertainment, but were more often considered to be healing medicines. Insights came to both the teller and the audience from the tales, which usually required a spiritual groundwork to be completed prior to, and following, the telling.

Many stories evolved out of adversity to show the nobility (or weakness) of the human spirit. These stories tell of experiences which can be your own, those of your family and friends, or drawn from the suffering of others in the immediate or global community.

Surprisingly, many of these old stories reveal special insights, truths and values which we desperately need in today's pressured and overstressed society. Many are 'trickster' stories showing us how change is brought about in our lives.

Stories such as 'Psyche and Eros' or 'Innana' and others, are used to rectify wrongs, teach understanding, assist in behavioural and attitude transformations, heal wounds (such as unresolved conflict and grief) and recreate lost memory.

People can be so traumatised by personal misfortunes and accidents and societal pressures that they are unable to release tensions and stresses which have built up within themselves and so they become ill. By working carefully with story we can show parallels to their predicament and, often, one of the many layers of the story will connect and suggest ways to resolve the problem.

Later, when encouraged to tell their own stories, the listeners recognise the causes of adversity in their lives and, looking from a different perspective, discover hidden solutions which help to begin the healing process. Helen often says, 'Whatever trauma has happened in your life, you have managed to survive. Merely having survived to tell the story is important. You're already living proof of success!'

Most people have deep within them the resources to heal themselves. The trauma they have experienced paralyses their ability to access this valuable resource. Therefore, the use of story is helpful in getting people through the paralysing pain and hurt feelings, enabling them to reach down into personal reservoirs and begin the healing processes and maybe even find answers to troubling questions.

In *Telling Makes it So*, Harriet Mason shows that using story as a metaphor can help people in a similar manner to our use of puppets to help children tell stories. By disassociating them and carefully leading them through the story several times, each time focussing on a different aspect, discoveries about and connections to the problems causing the distress in their lives are made.

Mason points out that 'Memories are stories we tell ourselves about the past and fears are stories we tell ourselves about the future. Together they influence how we interpret the present.'

Storytelling is a valuable aid in the social management of many problems. For those children who fear separation from their parents when they start school for the first time, who need to go into hospital, or even, whose parents are about to separate or divorce, stories can help allay many of their fears. Events or issues that might threaten or unsettle the child in real life can be explored in the non-threatening context of the story told by a trustworthy, caring adult and so prepare the child for the difficulties, challenges and changes that lie ahead.

Storytelling is used in grief, marriage and other relationship (especially family) counselling, with homeless children, or children who have suffered domestic violence or sexual abuse. In most cases of these latter types of abuse, the affected children feel so guilty and frightened of further violence, if they reveal the details of the abuse, that they attempt to block them out. Consequently, these children function at levels well below normal and, today, as teachers and other associates recognise the symptoms, suspicions of abuse are quickly raised.

Be aware that this is a specialist field; only people trained specifically in this counselling should attempt this work. Stories have been developed with the potential for healing these psychologically wounded children. *Once Upon a Time: Therapeutic Stories to Heal Abused Children*, by Nancy Davis, is a good example (see *Bibliography*).

Recently, at the Book Fair at Darling Harbour in Sydney, we found an excellent series of colourful story books specially developed by Liz Farrington, a behavioural therapist, to help children understand their emotions. Series titles and their associated emotions include:

Painting the Fire; (anger); *Red Poppies For a Little Bird* (guilt); *And Peter Said Goodbye* (grief); T*anya and the Green-eyed Monster* (jealousy); *Rainbow Fields* (loneliness); *Nightmare in the Mist* (fear); and *William's Gift* (hurt). Each of these books is accompanied by an excellent children's workbook and a parents' guide.

Storytelling is utilised to help people suffering from certain psychological or physical disorders. It is frequently used to build a better understanding of community problems. People suffering from substance addictions, such as drug and alcohol abuse, benefit greatly when they are able to use story to discover and explain the causes of their problems. Often answers are found in the wisdom buried deep in the layers of these stories.

Counselling with story is often used in the workplace, to settle issues and maintain harmonious relationships. This use of story eases the feelings of confrontation in disputes. In this way everyone involved in the dispute maintains their self-esteem and wins.

Stories build bridges

Storytelling is very useful in bridging the gap between the cultures of the world. Although we were continually bombarded with graphic material on our television screens during the course of the Vietnam war, a recent outing to see the musical *Miss Saigon* gave me and others in our party a greater understanding of the Vietnamese people's suffering. The storyline was superb and so effective. Truth was dressed up as parable and the message was received.

People who have immigrated from other countries can tell their stories to help build acceptance and a sense of personal value in their new community. Their stories add a new and different flavour, helping to enrich the culture and develop understanding amongst the community they have adopted. This is especially useful in the classroom.

Where a foreign student is having difficulty with the new language, the teacher may ask the class to make up a story in which all the 'power words' are in the language of the newcomer. Alternatively the class could go on an imaginative journey to the newcomer's country of origin. The story of this journey allows the foreign student to participate by translating common phrases and values for the rest of the class, giving the newcomer an enhanced sense of self-esteem.

There are so many great stories from overseas out there in the community just waiting and needing to be told. *Schindler's Ark*, a story told to Thomas Kenneally by a Polish immigrant, later became the classic film *Schindler's List*, which is now helping our younger generation understand the lessons and horrors of the Jewish Holocaust of World War II. This knowledge may even help prevent a similar occurrence during their lives — such is the power of story.

In our New South Wales Storytelling Guild we welcome people from all cultures to come and tell their stories. When this type of sharing occurs, everyone in the guild gains in knowledge and understanding. Through storytelling we can all learn how to communicate with each other again and to break down many of the current social barriers.

Selection of the stories used in therapy and in building bridges is critical. Make sure the stories you use are sensitive to the needs and feelings of your listeners or audiences and will reinforce their self-esteem.

Books for understanding storytelling as a healing mechanism

Estés, Clarissa Pinkola, *Women who Run with the Wolves*. Gives classic examples and explanations of the way the stories she uses can heal wounds. We highly recommend this book.

Davis, Nancy. *Once Upon a Time*: *Therapeutic Stories to Heal*

Abused Children. Information available through National Story-telling Association (NAPPS), P.O.Box 309, Jonesborough, Tenn. 37659, USA.

Mason, Harriet. *Telling Makes it So: The Use of Storytelling in Counselling.* Transcription of the set of 3 audio cassette tapes, Lincoln Publishing Inc., Lake Oswego, Oregon, 1994.

Specialist book series for children about emotions

Each book in this series is accompanied by a parents' guide and a separate workbook for children. They are available through most retail outlets, or inquiries may be made to Specialist Publications, phone 02 9736 2191.

Anger
Sherwood, Jonathon, *Painting the Fire* (Concept by Liz Farrington), Enchanté Publications, 1995.

Guilt
Sherwood, Jonathon, *Red Poppies For a Little Bird*, (Concept by Liz Farrington), Enchanté Publications, 1995.

Grief
Weil, Jennifer, *And Peter Said Goodbye*, (Concept by Liz Farrington), Enchanté Publications, 1995.

Jealousy
Sherwood, Jonathon, *Tanya and the Green-eyed Monster*, (Concept by Liz Farrington), Enchanté Publications, 1995.

Loneliness
Goldman-Rubin, Susan, *Rainbow Fields*, (Concept by Liz Farrington), Enchanté Publications, 1995.

Fear
McGuire, Leslie, *Nightmare in the Mist*, (Concept by Liz Farrington), Enchanté Publications, 1995.

Hurt
Weil, Jennifer, *William's Gift*, (Concept by Liz Farrington), Enchanté Publications, 1995.

12 The World's Greatest Teachers Used Stories

THE world's greatest teachers used stories to get their messages across. Spiritual tales from diverse religious persuasions will add variety and spice to your storytelling repertoire. There is a rich literature of Christian parables, Hasidic tales, and stories from the Buddhist, Zen Buddhist, Sufi, Hindu, Islamic, Aboriginal and Confucian traditions. Often they expose the 'trickster' or rascal element at work in the community and give us significant warnings or spiritual guidance.

These stories may illuminate our relationship to others, encourage us to show compassion, create a sense of wonder, or sanction the concept of togetherness. They provoke us to wonder about who we are and why we are here and give us insights to the meaning of life.

Many of the greatest teachers never actually wrote down their stories themselves. They taught their followers and it was left to others to record these special stories. There are wonderful tales, relating to every philosophy and culture in the world which have stood the test of time. Even today they are the stepping stones to spiritual enlightenment.

The values that are central to these stories still speak to our audiences today and still are relevant to modern-day life. Their spirituality shows there is more to life than what we can see, touch and hear. A story may show our connection to the universe, the planet, other earthly species and other people.

Although humans claim they only want to hear the truth, they frequently react to it with hostility. Knowing this, the great religious teachers dressed up the truth and wrapped it in the form of parable, fable, or stories, to make it more acceptable to the masses.

This point was cleverly illustrated by David Kossoff in his book, *Small Town is a World*, with the parable 'The Story About Parable — Twin Brother of Truth'. Parable was fun to be with. He was always beautifully dressed and was invited everywhere, but people were shocked and frightened by naked Truth and made him unwelcome. This enlightening parable is reprinted in Charles Arcodia's *Stories for Sharing* (see *Bibliography*). Get a copy if you can and read it. The book includes some lovely small pieces, ready for telling.

Jesus Christ, Buddha, Confucius and other great philosophers used story, in the form of parables, to teach and convey their messages. A *parable* is a story with both a literal and a hidden meaning. It is a fictitious story told to point a moral. A well-known example is Jesus Christ's parable of 'The Prodigal Son', from the Gospels of the New Testament.

Jesus Christ told many stories in the form of parables to teach his followers about some of the more complex and important life values and to engender a belief in God, the Father. They are to be found in the Gospels of the New Testament and are still relevant today. Children and grown-ups everywhere still remain fascinated by these simple Bible stories.

We can all recall some of the stories which taught us lessons in our childhood — Aesop's *Fables*, for example. A fable is a story not based on fact. It is a short, simple moral tale, often using animals as its characters.

Aesop was a Greek slave who lived in 600 BC. Each of his brief tales offers advice cloaked in a simple, humorous way, about human virtues and failings. The characters Aesop uses in his stories are animals who talk, think and act like humans. These stories are as pertinent today as they were when they were written.

Listed below. are some examples of Aesop's many fables and their lessons:

- 'The crow and the fox' teaches about vanity.
- 'The lion and the mouse' teaches not to judge people by their appearance.
- 'The fox and the sick lion' teaches you to think for yourself.
- 'The goose that laid the golden egg' teaches about greed.
- 'The boy who cried "Wolf"' shows nobody believes a liar, even when he tells the truth.
- 'The hare and the tortoise' shows that slow but sure wins the race.

Fairytales such as the tales of the Brothers Grimm still play a large part in the education and enjoyment of the children of the world. Their continuing relevance is indicated by the fact that many of these stories have been the basis of recent excellent children's films.

The sub-text of these tales, which have educated and entertained generations of children, contains great wisdom and teaches important values. They reveal some of the harsher aspects of European history and the darker realms of human psychology as in 'The Pied Piper' and 'Hansel and Gretel'.

Many people feel concerned that some of the old folk tales and fairytales cause children to become fearful. This is not so. Today's psychologists suggest that these stories identify the deep fears we all have and bring them to the surface where they can be dealt with in a healthy way and in a secure environment.

Hans Christian Andersen, who died in 1875, was Denmark's most famous author. His fairytales are among the most widely read works in world literature and his stories reassure children that good does indeed triumph over evil, and that persistence, hard work and other virtues are rewarded.

As many of these traditional tales are couched in outdated language and come to us through translations, you may want to go back to the original source of the story that you wish to tell, read different versions of it and rewrite it in today's language before you tell it.

If you do attempt this, be true to the spirit of the story. Recently a friend tried to 'sanitise' a story by replacing a fairly violent scene with a peaceful, though less-satisfying resolution. The class totally rubbished her new version, preferring instead the old version they knew well and which made more sense to them.

Take care that any alterations you make to a story are in keeping with the messages in the original story. Do remember — children are intelligent young people who like their literature to be lively, energetic and full-blooded, not watered down and 'safe'.

Stories to build attitudes

Many people are confident that attitudes can be changed by stories. Dr Margaret Read MacDonald, storyteller and researcher, says in *Peace Tales*, published in 1992:

> In studying the world's folktales I have come to the conclusion that these tales present a mirror of the mind of mankind . . . Throughout history and wherever humans reside on this planet, their tales speak repeatedly of the same concern and reach similar conclusions. In the past, mankind's tales stressed trickery and power more often than conflict resolution. Is it possible that, by changing the tales we tell, we can change our warring natures? It is worth a try.

Makes you think, doesn't it? Aren't we constantly reinforcing the negativity we find so prevalent in today's society by the stories we read in the print media, listen to on radio broadcasts and watch on TV in the lounge rooms of our homes?

The answer from the media barons is that bad news 'sells better' than good news, so little wonder that we are constantly bombarded with it. The effect on our society is currently being

monitored by psychologists, concerned about the rise in violent behaviour and the seeming desensitisation of the public to these types of negative attitudes. Could offering more positively directed stories reverse some of this damage to our social fabric?

Dr Philip Cam, Senior Lecturer in Philosophy and foundation Chair of the Federation of Australasian Philosophy for Children Associations, has recently published a series of 'thinking stories' for children. The *Thinking Stories* readers and activity/resource books are designed to encourage children 'to question, to see consequences', and 'to search for meaning, enriching and extending their understanding'. (Dr Cam's books are listed in the *Bibliography*.)

Charles Arcodia's *Stories for Sharing* contains 54 delightful stories drawn from Christian, Buddhist, Hindu, Chinese, Sufi, Hasidic and modern-day parables, with suggestions for group discussions and further reading on each topic. For those looking for stories with moral themes to share with others, we recommend it.

Look again at the stories from the great teachers. I'm sure you will find value and relevance in their messages.

13 Story Selection

WHICH comes first: the chicken or the egg? Should you first consider the story or the audience to which it will be told? We believe it is the audience which is the most important component.

Before you start browsing through books for stories to tell at your next presentation, consider your audience: what will best suit it; what are its preferences likely to be.

Some people prefer storytelling to children, while others can't stand the little ankle-biters and present before adult audiences only. Try telling simple stories in front of all types of audiences and establish where your preferences and special abilities lie. Remember . . . everyone is different.

Many people spend more time selecting the story when they should give more time and energy to finding out about the audience for whom it will be targeted. Knowing something about your audience makes selection of the story easier.

What is the purpose of the storytelling event? It is not just a question of grabbing any story and hoping it will be OK. Selection is about searching out the right story, and matching it up to fit your audience.

Warning: take care. Often when stories are told as part of a speaker's presentation, the stories selected are totally unsuitable for the messages they are to convey — or even — the intended audience.

Think of the way some political and other leaders have upset their supporters by the choice of an offensive off-colour story or joke more suitable for the footy change-room than a public meeting. Poor selection of a story has cost these people popularity, respect and even their job.

So, once you have identified your audience, you must decide what types of stories you will feel comfortable telling. To help you make your selection, try first to identify the purpose of your storytelling. Is it to educate, entertain, to make people aware of history, religion, social issues, politics or, to recount personal experiences? Having identified these points, finding appropriate stories to tell will be much more straightforward.

Selecting which story to present is critical, so:

1. *Research your audience.*
- Is your story suitable for the group you are targeting?
- Is it suitable for your style of telling?
- Are the messages strong and positive?
- Will your story offend?

2. *Choose a story you like — one which speaks to you.*
- Do you feel a passion to tell it?
- Emphasise the bits *you* like.
- Leave out the boring bits which slow it down.
- Craft it carefully, to give it an aesthetically pleasing shape.
- Make sure your message fits the story, or in other words, that the story is able to carry the message.

3. *Visualise the story.*
- Picture the story in your mind to help you better communicate it to your audience. Unless you can see the action clearly in your mind, you'll have difficulty communicating it in words to an audience.

4. *Practise the story out aloud.*
- Tape it and play it back so you can correct or prune out anything that affects the rhythm.
- Listen to how it sounds, using the images you visualise in your head.
- Make any necessary changes to reinforce those images.
- Retape the corrected version of the story.

5. *Learn it by heart* and *practise until you know it well*.
- Work from the structure rather than trying to be word perfect.
- Add flesh to your skeleton to round it out and make it come alive. Each telling is different, depending on how the audience reacts to the story and how you respond to the audience. You will never tell a story the same way twice, so learn the structure and then 'flesh it out'.

7. *Always have a range of stories in your repertoire.*
- When you arrive at the venue you may find the story you have chosen is not suitable.
- Try not to offend. Storytellers of all kinds must be flexible; ready for any contingency.

If you wish to make use of a story in a speech presentation:

1. Make your point.
2. Tell an appropriate story to illustrate your point.
3. Show the relevance of the story, or point, to the audience's lives.

Be passionate

In order to grab and hold your audience's attention you must be enthusiastic about your chosen story. Recall those stories which have left a deep impression on you and look for tales that evoke a similar response or that have a similar style. If you like the story and feel a passion about telling it, you can be assured of success. Margaret Read MacDonald suggests in *The Storyteller's Start-up Book*:

> Don't waste your time on material that doesn't inspire an eagerness to tell. And it might take quite a search to find a handful of those gems that feel 'just right' for your telling.

Your chosen story may be in a literary format, not immediately suitable for telling. To make it more accessible to an audience it will need some reworking. If you intend telling professionally and you choose a modern story protected by copyright, *permission must be obtained* from the author and publisher.

Note that there are some cultures, such as that of the Australian Aborigines, which regard their traditional folk tales as 'copyright property'. For instance, Australian Aboriginal Dreamtime stories are now copyright material. Check that you do not infringe their tribal rights.

How to choose

How do you choose from among the many variants of traditional stories? Margaret Read MacDonald's *The Storyteller's Source Book* is an invaluable tool in making this selection. It lists all the known variants of traditional stories. The Cinderella story, for instance, has hundreds of variants, crossing many cultural borders. Certain stories are common to many cultures. By consulting a source book, you can easily identify and select whichever version of any tale you wish to tell.

Make sure you have a wide selection of stories in your repertoire ready for presentation. As you come across new stories, adapt and refine them to suit your telling style, so that they are accessible when you need them. Remember, not all stories are suitable for all types of audience.

Wrap your message in a story

Getting your message across and making it memorable is important to most of us in our working lives and not just to those who identify themselves as storytellers.

Writers, poets, librarians, actors, dancers, mime artists, pup-
peteers, public speakers, politicians, parents, grandparents,
advertising executives, church leaders, doctors, nurses, lawyers,
sales-people, secretaries, accountants and teachers — all require
the storyteller's skill. All of these people use the vehicle of story
to get their message across as part of their daily work. Messages
cloaked in a good story are always remembered; without the
vehicle of story, ideas and words are often lost.

A good example of this is a parcel which you may have
received for Mother's Day or a birthday. Parcel Number One is
given the way I often receive them . . . untidily thrown together
and hastily stuck down with tape. (Does this sound familiar?)
They're usually still in the plastic carry bag, complete with the
docket. Not very exciting, is it?

But, I guess I was lucky to get anything at all. Doesn't say
that the gift-giver didn't care for me, but that rather, having
bought the gift, they couldn't be bothered taking the time to
make any further effort.

Parcel Number Two shows the recipient that someone cares
about the gift, has taken a little time and trouble to create an
illusion which will make it memorable. The carefully fitted paper
wrapping, matching ribbon and decorative bow, with delicate
orchids entwined in it, tells us something about the giver.

The first parcel reminds us of those advertisements on radio
and television, which are gabbled through at such a fast clip that
the company should not have bothered. Most of the message is
lost. The listener gives up trying to keep pace and loses interest.
You know what I mean, we've all seen them or heard them on
television. Would you trust their product?

The second parcel reminds us of those advertisements which stimulate listeners or viewers by
catching their attention with a simple story wrapped
attractively (often humorously) around the message. It clearly
demonstrates a level of caring.

The story you wrap around your message should fit perfectly

and must catch the interest of your audience. I remember several advertisements from years ago, whose messages remained memorable, because of the stories they employed.

For instance: the beer advertisements, in particular, the hilariously funny neighbourhood working bee, building a garage; or the fishing contest, with entries of half-frozen fish covered with bits of newspaper. Do you remember an airline travel advertisement about a father returning home from a long business trip; or, lately, some of the telephone advertisements, which make you want to respond immediately to their message? When I see or hear these story advertisements, I have an irrepressible urge to pick up the phone immediately and call my family in New Zealand.

These advertisements were crafted to suit both the product and the potential consumers. Many of the successful ones move us and entertain us. Their messages 'got through' in large part due to the vehicle of story. I remembered the stories and therefore the messages they carried.

So — select your stories carefully to fit whatever audience you are to present to and you will be successful.

14 Where to Find Stories

As mentioned previously, selection of the 'right' story for your particular audience's needs is very important. There are millions of stories from which you can choose, between the pages of books in libraries, archives, book stores, especially second-hand book stores, or even garage sales. Other people's experiences and your own personal life is a rich repository of story. Pull out family heirlooms, photos, letters. Investigate your family tree.

Ask some of your ageing family members to explain family stories (about both the 'good' and the 'bad' family members). You will be surprised just what some of your family elders can tell you. They may be humorous, happy or sad stories, of good or evil deeds. You may find absolute gems once you start delving. Remember, Australia was a 'special' settlement and people came here (or were transported) for a host of reasons — all of which makes for more stories.

If you have no aged family members, go to some of the

retirement villages or nursing homes. The people living there have some of the most incredible tales to pass on. If they don't mind, record these tales for future use. Get their permission first and then *record them now* before the people pass away and the stories are lost forever.

Storytelling is truly a sharing experience

Librarians will be delighted to help you find where the kind of stories you need are located. Go to your local library and browse through the shelves in the appropriate sections. Myths and legends, folklore, stories from other cultures, Bible stories and other religious or philosophical works will all provide grist for your mill.

Archives are wonderful places in which to find material for stories — so much information about our past is accumulated there. Check out old diaries, letters, family photograph albums. Stories can be found everywhere. Select the ones that talk to you.

How to fit stories to your audience

Whenever people get together, they swap stories about things that happened in their lives. Some of the most popular stories told are personal ones. Tell the stories which will evoke memories of similar experiences in the lives of your audience. They are always the most successful.

Use common everyday expressions as vehicles to build your stories. Think of Aunty's 'got a bone in my leg', whenever she didn't want to do something. When asked by a child about her age, 'as old as my tongue and just a bit older than my teeth', or the 'lower than a red-bellied black snake' and 'off like a bucket of prawns in the sun' responses. These allow a great opportunity for the audience to identify with the expressions and relate to their own experiences. Develop these stories in a way that draws your audience closer to you.

As discussed earlier it is crucial that you find out as much as you can in advance about the audience. Phone the club's secretary, read any literature, attend a meeting incognito, if you need to, but find out what their interests are. The information you gather will help you to select and adapt your stories to suit the audience.

Don't attempt to excuse yourself later with 'I misread my audience'. When offended, audiences can be most unforgiving. Do your research first, so everyone can enjoy the experience.

Because we tailored our stories to suit the specific needs of our young sight-impaired audience, our session with them worked out very successfully. We realised that visual methods and the use of gestures and other body language would be of little use in this case, and so we came prepared to use other methods to communicate our stories to our audience.

Think carefully about what you can do to meet the special needs and expectations of your audience. Look at your stories and analyse them. This will help you to understand better how they work and make it easy to present each story in a way that will give audience satisfaction. Take the time to get it right.

15 *Adapting to Oral Forms*

NOT all stories are immediately ready for telling. As many are written in a literary style, they are often wordy and use passive, outdated language and indirect or reported (rather than direct and dramatisable) speech. This slows up the pace of the story and risks boring the listeners.

Storytelling requires the use of fast-paced, active language to give the story a sense of forward momentum and excitement. Find a story you really like and go through it, pruning out any unnecessary, old-fashioned language, adjectives and adverbs; design it to suit your style of telling. You need to get it into a shape that suits you and your audience.

A number of popular old stories (such as the Beatrix Potter classics, a favourite among children), need to be adapted for telling to today's children. I'm sure you can think of many of your favourite stories which will need the language updated before presenting to an audience.

It is really difficult for a beginner to know how best to convert a literary story into an oral form. Initially, novice storytellers should select tales already prepared for telling. This will provide them with a formula or style to emulate.

There are many books available nowadays containing stories which are ideal for oral use. Look around the libraries and bookshops to find these. If the stories are written in fast-paced direct language they'll be suitable for telling.

If you decide to rewrite a traditional story for today's audiences, or if you write your own stories for storytelling, the story will require:

1. A strongly defined theme and carefully crafted plot.
2. Good characterisation. Make your characters sound alive and believable.
3. Lots of action — have a strong forward momentum. Keep the story moving along at a fast pace — both in the text and dialogue.
4. Try to avoid flashbacks, which stop the forward momentum and interrupt the flow.
5. Lots of action. Try not to discuss the thoughts and attitudes of your characters. Instead, *show* how they feel through their actions and words.
6. Build the conflict to an almost impossible height.
7. Then solve the dilemma and end it quickly.
8. The fast ending may have a twist built in. Audiences love a surprise ending.

 If you feel it is necessary to start at a high point in the drama, do so. However, so you don't lose the momentum of the drama, it is better to have no more than one flashback. This way, you can go back to the beginning and explain how the story came to pass, using the heightening conflict to build tension.

Finish quickly with the resolution and ending. When using a flashback keep the language fast-paced and build the conflict to an almost unbearably high pitch.

If you are using someone else's story you may wish to change the point of view, maybe even change the sex of the main characters. Changes to the time frame or setting could create a novel approach. Many traditional tales have enjoyed renewed popularity when set in modern times.

Minor characters may be added to round out the action, provide a sub-plot, or you may decide to eliminate some to simplify and strengthen the story. You may decide to lengthen the story to add to the tension and conflict or, maybe, cuts could be made to eliminate sections which slow down the action.

Practise and refine

Practise and continue to refine your chosen story in subsequent tellings to friends and family. Read and record your story on to a tape and listen to it objectively.

Cut out or alter any words or passages, such as 'she said' or 'he replied'. Use different voices for your characters. Eliminate other phrases which affect the rhythm and cause you to stumble. There are always simple alternatives to replace the long, awkward phrases which trip you up. Try to make your sentences short, snappy ones.

Retape the story. Keep on playing and refining it until you are happy with the result.

Once you are satisfied with the shape and form and you know it well, the story is ready to present to an audience. Try telling it again to some close friends, family, or people who will give you an honest evaluation.

All the practice and refining processes should help you to learn the story off by heart and to tell it that much better. Create your vision of it and use the pictures in your mind to tell your story more vividly.

Let the audience join in

If you enjoy the pleasure of interaction with your audience, don't forget to write some audience participation responses into your story. To help the audience remember them more easily, try to make these phrases simple, incorporating in them a strong rhythm. No audience is too sophisticated to become involved in group responses.

Whenever Helen mentions the volcano in her story 'Bill and the Miracle of the Fish', the audience responds with: 'It went Crash, it went Bang; it roared and it shrieked! It went Crash, it went Bang; it roared and it shrieked!' People who participate in the response love the rhythm and look forward to the next opportunity to join in. Listening for the next cue to participate also operates to keep the audience alert and focussed on the story.

We have used interactive storytelling successfully with young children, teenagers, adults, business people, and senior audiences. All seem to enjoy being involved with a part of the story. (For further reading on interactive telling, see the *Bibliography*.)

Look around your community for stories you can adapt to your style of telling and to develop your storytelling skills further. Personal stories from your life journey are the very best.

Learning a story

You have found the right story for telling, but how do you learn it?

Learning by rote is not the only solution. Let's consider two basic approaches to learning a story.

1. *The visual approach*

With this approach the story is seen in the mind of the teller as a series of pictures. The storyteller 'sees' the action taking place and uses the pictures to add credibility and give deeper meaning as the story unfolds.

To help reinforce the images in your mind you can draw up a simple storyboard sequence of events. Storyboarding consists of drawing up a series of small boxes into which you sketch each significant event as it occurs in your story. (The drawings need not be masterpieces; stick figures will suffice.) Storyboarding will identify any weaknesses in the structure making it relatively easy to reinforce and improve these weak areas.

Another visual technique is to practise your story in front of a mirror (or video camera, if you are lucky enough to own one), so you can see what your body language is like. It is easier to alter any unsatisfactory gestures when you are first learning the story, than later, when you have developed bad habits.

To help impress the words in your mind, highlight paragraphs and key phrases in the text with different coloured highlighting pens. This method of using colour impresses the words and key phrases firmly in your memory.

2. *The auditory approach*

In order to learn by hearing, tell the story out aloud or into a tape-recorder and concentrate on how your voice sounds.

You will find it instructive to play back your story when you are free from noisy interruptions. Play it at night, as you are about to go to sleep, and again in the morning as you awaken. Play it in the car, when you are travelling any distance and, wherever possible, join in along with the tape. Practising it frequently helps to fix it in your memory. Adapt the story where the language sounds awkward or clumsy and then retape the adaptation. The *auditory approach* assists the storyteller to remember key structures, repetitive phrases and choruses in the story.

Know the structure fully, so you can add 'the flesh to the bones' more easily. Practise telling the story from the inside out until it comes to mind naturally. You don't have to learn the words off perfectly; no two tellings or audiences are exactly the same. The story will evolve with each telling.

Following these suggestions will help make your storytelling more enjoyable. Enjoyment is the name of the game.

16 Endings

S TRONG endings are as important as beginnings. They are a vital part of the story's framework. Your ending should satisfy the listener. It is at the end of the story that all the conflicts are resolved, the questions are answered and the tension which has built up to an intense climax is released.

There are many varied ways in which to end your story, but it must remain consistent with the characters and their actions throughout your tale. This is not to say that the ending must be predictable or can't be interesting. On the contrary.

Helen's story 'The Golden Threads' uses the well-tried formula of the 'happy-ever-after' ending:

> *Quickly she released her white dove, which flew upwards, wheeling round and round, climbing higher and higher. As the tiny speck finally disappeared into the clear blue sky they heard from far away the low rumble of thunder. At the sound of the thunder, the Prince quickly scooped the damsel up in his arms, carrying her across the threshold into a new life, in which they lived happily ever after.*

Audiences — be they either children or adult audiences — find this ending satisfactory and Helen is often asked to repeat this story.

Happy endings aren't compulsory; some sad endings are just

right, providing they fit the characters and story. For instance, the baddie may get his 'just deserts' as the loose ends are all finally tidied up.

Or maybe, you can have a ten-hanky ending where the heroine dies after overcoming impossible odds during the story. These sad endings are just as satisfying for the listeners as, with their tears, they release the tension built up in the conflict of the story.

The end to your story could leave a hook to bring the audience back for a further story in the series or to see what happens next. Then there's the humorous ending where the tension is resolved with laughter. I cannot think of a better way in which to end a story.

Alternatively you can end your story with a twist. You've set your audience up to expect a particular style of ending — perhaps a 'happy ever after' — but instead, you leave them with a question, allowing them to resolve what happens next for themselves. Be aware that this style of ending must be executed carefully or it could weaken the story's impact.

One of the important elements at the end of your story is to show the changes which the protagonist has undergone. The audience needs to be brought full circle or clearly shown the difference between the situation at the beginning and how it is at the end. This comparison could be happy or sad, tragic or comic, depending on your type of story. What you must remember is that your audience must feel satisfied that the ending was the right one.

Try to allow your characters and their actions to direct the end rather than leaving the final resolution to external circumstances such as a storm, accident or other act of God. Leaving your ending in the lap of the gods is a poor way to finish and will probably feel like a disappointment or even a cheat to your listeners.

Plot out your story so that your ending is a strong one. Alter the words of a traditional tale to achieve a more satisfying result.

Make sure the final picture in the series is complete for the listeners. That is part of your artistry as a storyteller.

Diane Wolkstein's Chinese tale, *White Wave* (1996), ends thus:

All that remained was the story.
But that's how it is with all of us.
When we die, all that remains is the story.

17 Stage Fright and Other Disasters

In storytelling, as in public speaking, untoward things happen—sometimes when you least expect them. Here are some hints which we have found helped us cope with these unhappy situations.

When your voice lets you down

You have a booking for a storytelling performance. You wake on the day; but when you try to speak your voice comes out as a whisper! It's too late to cancel and you can't reach any fellow storytellers who could replace you. What to do?

Be positive. You get up and gargle with everything suitable in the bathroom cabinet, drink sumptuous quantities of lemon and honey, suck every lozenge you can afford, but still, hours later, your voice is merely a hoarse whisper. Finally you decide you will have to show up and try to make the best of it. Here are some devices to ease a difficult situation.

Use a good microphone. If you don't possess a mike, check whether the venue has one you can use, or if necessary, hire one from a sound system supplier. Make sure it is working well and try it out before you start. We have our own microphones — ones we know we can rely on.

Tell your audience that your throat is in trouble; they'll understand. Most people have experienced this problem at some time during their lives. Give them a signal when you are about to speak (use a rain-stick) so the room quickly becomes very quiet. If possible, get the person introducing you to make the audience aware of your predicament.

Whisper, 'I have a little more voice than this, but not much, so I need your help.' People will want to help you when they see you are genuinely in trouble.

Have a drink of warmish water beside you to prevent your throat from drying out. Avoid iced water, it will only make matters worse.

Encourage your audience to participate. Tell stories which will allow them to enjoy helping you.

Keep a sense of humour. Laugh at the funny sounds you make and the audience will relax with you.

Play an instrument or use more music in your storytelling to give your voice a chance to rest for a moment.

Tie the theme of your lost voice into a personal experience story and the audience will identify and empathise with you. (Prepare in advance for this sort of event by having a story you can use in your repertoire.)

By using your brain, you can get yourself out of this type of awkward situation without damaging your reputation. The scout motto applies here: 'Be Prepared'.

Here's a friend's recipe that has been tried and tested and could work for you:

Take a root of ginger and a whole garlic bulb, roughly chopped, add three or four cut up lemons, honey to sweeten and cover with water. Boil for 45 minutes, keeping the water topped up, strain and cool. Drink frequently.

See a doctor as soon as you are able and get specialist help for your voice. It is your most valuable tool.

Stage fright

Everyone is nervous to start with. A touch of nerves is not a bad thing so long as it adds an edge to your performance and doesn't get in the way or prevent you from doing your best. Stage fright is a normal reaction for a novice speaker or teller. Develop some 'magical' aids to set the scene and help keep your 'butterflies' under control. A story hat, cape, magic carpet, wishing candle, or costume — all of these could help overcome the ogre that is stage fright. We have found that using puppets helps to focus both the audience's and your attention on the story.

Learn your story off by heart so you don't need to use notes. If you are worried about forgetting your lines take along some small, easy-to-handle prompt cards as a security blanket — just in case.

If you forget a part, or leave a bit out, you can always say, 'Oh, by the way . . .', and then insert the forgotten piece. Using a conspiratorial tone, you can always say, 'You may not have known this, but . . .' and include the missing information. One of Gail Herman's helpful phrases is, 'You see . . .' She teaches her students to repeat the last phrase or sentence and to elaborate, if they forget where they are in the story. You could use the audience as a prompt by asking them what they have learned so far. Be innovative.

If your knees are shaky, sit down on a chair or stool to tell, and have the audience seated close together on the floor, in front of you. Seating them together will develop common bonds and they will respond better to your story. Smile and your audience will warm to you and smile back. That return smile will ease your nerves.

Telling stories in pairs can bolster a nervous speaker's confidence. Each teller supports the other and can act as a prompt or 'ad lib', where a line may be forgotten. Props, like puppets, can help a novice to settle, providing something other than 'self' on which to concentrate. When you first go out storytelling, it is best to choose what is — for you — the least daunting audience: a smallish group of young children or, whatever.

Other disasters

Recently when a group of us were promoting the Storytelling Guild and telling some stories at a church function we had an experience all performers dread.

Having totally enjoyed the interactive story, an elderly gent in his mid eighties collapsed at a table in front of Helen. Although asked to keep going, she stopped, as many people sprang up to help with the emergency. The audience's attention was on the drama occurring in their midst as they watched those assisting lay him in the aisle and perform CPR (emergency resuscitation) on him.

Fortunately, the organiser called a coffee break. Over the next ten minutes everyone calmed down. Helen wandered round making contact with the audience and re-bonding with them during the break.

While they drank their coffee the audience had time to settle so that, when we recommenced, Helen had their full attention. The drama over, she re-presented the piece she'd been telling when the interruption occurred. By the way, happily the gentleman recovered and was driven home.

Children's capers

Children in your audience don't always make life easy either. Helen was in the midst of telling her first story when a two-year old ran out, stood right in front of her and started to slow clap. As the audience's attention was being distracted by this unofficial performance, Helen stopped at the end of a sentence and gave the child the recognition she sought. Satisfied, she ran back to her Mum and Helen was able to continue.

At another telling, a child who'd volunteered to 'cry like a baby' decided she'd rather 'moo' like a cow and, following that, stood there for some minutes saying 'Ribbit ribbit', like a frog. The teller stopped, let the audience applaud the child and continued with the story. Having received the recognition she sought, the child stayed on the stage but was quiet after that.

When storytelling down at the Mitchell Library, Berice was interrupted by a drunk. He'd listened to her story of 'The Little Red House', in which an apple represents the house in the story, fixed her with a red-eyed gaze and suddenly broke in with, 'Thatch's not a little red house . . . thatch's a napple.' Berice quickly acknowledged his comment and, with a smile, continued the story without further interruption.

Handling a heckler

Should you have the misfortune to encounter a heckler, rather than ignoring the interruption, ask the person to stand and repeat what they've said. *Keeping the heckler standing*, throw the comment out to the audience, asking for a solution.

Get one or two opinions from the audience and, when you are satisfied with the replies, refer the matter back to the heckler, who should still be standing up. Should the response not be satisfactory, arrange to discuss the issue later and continue your story, repeating the sentence or paragraph in which you were interrupted.

It is important in all of these various instances that you are seen to maintain control of the situation throughout its passage and that you keep your continuity, wherever possible.

When any of these incidents occur, don't freeze. Be aware that they can happen to anyone, without warning. Work out a strategy in advance which you can follow at the time you are interrupted. Without encouraging the heckler acknowledge them — that's usually all they want — and maintain control yourself.

Once again: 'BE PREPARED'.

18 Target Audiences for Stories

IF you are going to be a storyteller you have to get out there — and *tell stories!*

The world is out there waiting for you and craving stories, but, where do you start? To whom do you tell your stories? How do you find an audience?

There are more groups, clubs, associations and schools having regular meetings, than there are speakers and storytellers to fill the need. So, first, you must decide to which kind of audience you wish to tell stories.

Once you have identified your target audience you will need to contact the groups you are interested in. You may be quite surprised to find that you have a wealth of potential audiences awaiting *you* the Storyteller. All you need is the courage to pick up the phone and make that first inquiry.

Of course, while you are learning your craft, you wouldn't expect a huge fee for your time. Going from 'free to fee' shouldn't take place until all the necessary skills are in place and you have a reasonable repertoire of stories.

You have to perfect your skills 'off Broadway', where the most you will expect would be a free dinner and, if you have to travel some distance, maybe travel expenses. You could, of course, be content to 'just enjoy' your popularity as a storyteller.

Travelling around and meeting a variety of interesting people is a lot of fun. It's even more satisfying to have small children at the local shopping centre enthusiastically pointing you out to Mum as 'The Storyteller'.

Some of the places you may find to tell stories are:

3–4 years Playgroups, pre-schools, kindergartens, Sunday schools, birthday parties.

5–12 years Primary schools, Sunday schools, sports and community clubs, birthday parties.

13–18 years High schools, colleges, teenage clubs and parties.

Adults Sports clubs and associations, Bible study groups, churches, universities, tertiary institutions.

Special needs groups Homes and day care centres for the disabled, nursing homes and clubs for the ageing, retirement villages, therapy groups, hospitals, health support groups, shoppers and Golden Age clubs.

Mixed family entertainment Church groups and youth groups, clubs of all types.

Corporate After-dinner entertainment, speaking engagements, workshops.

Many of these audience possibilities can be found in the Yellow Pages under the headings — 'Community Organisations', 'Education — Preschools', 'Playgroups or Schools', 'Associations or Clubs', 'Religious Organisations', 'Retirement Villages', 'Nursing Homes', etc; from lists supplied by your local council or library, or health promotion units. Some public relations firms are interested in new talent, so phone up and offer your services.

Dial the contact numbers of a range of groups (bearing in mind the travelling distance) and enquire if they would be interested in using your special skills. You may get a few refusals, but you will be surprised how many will show interest in what you offer.

Place small fliers in local schools, churches, on the notice board at the local library and shopping centres. Apex, Lions,

Probus, View, Rotary and dozens of other clubs are always looking for interesting and entertaining speakers. Offer to tell them some of your stories.

These community service clubs don't usually pay but, you'll be fed (if it's a dinner meeting). We've eaten a lot of chicken dinners along the way to becoming professional. If your performance is good, and the word is passed around the community, paid work will eventually come to you. Word-of-mouth advertising is the very best kind.

19 *Business Matters*

C ONGRATULATIONS! You have completed your 'apprentice-
ship' along the way and have now decided to step out
and become a professional storyteller. We know this is a
major decision and so what follows are some helpful hints you
should consider when starting business.

Remember you don't have to reinvent the wheel — there is
help out there. Join organisations such as Storyteller's Guilds,
Toastmasters, ITC, National Speakers' Associations or other relevant groups where there are skilled people, very willing to share
their knowledge and expertise. Ask for their help and reap the
benefits of their experience and wisdom.

Having a certificate of accreditation from one or more of these
organisations would be of immense assistance in establishing
your credibility to a client organisation. Acquiring accreditation
with the Department of School Education is essential to gaining
work in Australian schools.

Nuts and bolts of business

Develop some quality promotional material to send to prospec-
tive clients. Obtain some well-designed business cards (with your
phone number clearly displayed), letterheads and information
pamphlets. Use good quality photographs and don't forget to

include some appropriate quotes from your testimonials under the heading 'What others say . . .'.

Keep a diary and use it daily. List in it the numbers of all phone calls you receive. Note all contacts and inquiries. Keep an up-to-date address book (never forgetting to note the all-important contact telephone number) and business card file.

Acquire a mileage book and list all travel costs relating to your storytelling activities (this includes research). Do this as well for all outgoing telephone calls. Keep a notebook of these so you can reclaim these costs. Collect receipts and claim expenses, such as subscriptions, costumes and equipment, stationery, photocopying, postage, printing, and other business expenses.

Seek some professional assistance to set up an accounting system which will help you keep track of your income, expenditure and such mind-boggling issues as tax matters.

When working in the community send media releases and community service announcements to local newspapers and radio stations. Offer local radio stations interview sessions and write articles about your storytelling work for magazines and newspapers. Contact organisations and offer your services free, to establish your name.

Be prepared to travel. The country areas are starved for visits of interesting city performers and, as we have found, country people are very hospitable.

 Always arrange for a testimonial on letterhead when finalising details of a presentation. And don't ever forget to send thank you letters for hospitality. This is all part of paying your dues on the way to a career.

Setting your fee

There are no specific guidelines as to how much you should ask for a storytelling session. When we started telling professionally in Sydney in the early 1990s we were paid a fee of $150 each per session. As our experience has expanded our fee has increased. Someone of the calibre of a Master or visiting international storyteller can receive $US 1,000 or more per session.

If you can, it helps to find out what budget the organisation engaging you has been allocated. You can negotiate from that point if the fee is insufficient for your needs.

Your storytelling experience will be a deciding factor when setting your fee structure. However, there are two major considerations:

1. Never sell your services too cheaply. People will regard this with suspicion.
2. Never ask exorbitant fees for your services. You won't get asked back if you do, especially if the expectations are not fulfilled.

Be realistic when setting your fees — you have to live. Put yourself in the hirer's shoes. Ask yourself how much you would pay someone with your skills. Set your fee at that level.

If your client organisation accepts the fee you suggest, go ahead and negotiate the details. As your workload expands gradually increase the fee, based on the number in the audience, the type of presentation and the time allocated.

An accountant advised me to base my fee on an absolute minimum of $100 per day to cover expenses. This was based on a breakdown of my budget. To this amount I added a further percentage which seems satisfactory to my clients.

Work out your own budget and find what your minimum income should be to cover your expenses. It's not an easy exercise but this will help you to establish a realistic fee structure.

Calculate how much time you will spend travelling to and from your venue, add an amount to cover a percentage of your development costs, any extra expenses you are required to cover (such as accommodation, mileage or travel, etc.) and how long your storytelling will take.

Ask for testimonials on letterheads stating whether or not the presentation was paid and keep a testimonial file of these. Photocopy these testimonials and use these copies as references when seeking work. Having this file to refer to shows how you have progressed in your career as a storyteller.

In our New South Wales Storytelling Guild we have an accreditation process which requires specific numbers of testimonials to be submitted for each of three levels of accreditation. Therefore it is important that you collect and file those testimonials.

Be professional in all your presentations and you will prosper.

Goodbye and Good Luck!

Having come this far, you are truly serious about your pursuit of storytelling excellence. Know that the only limits to your success are those you impose on yourself.

Step out boldly and with confidence. You bring a unique perspective to your craft.

Listen to everyone. Take what you find personally useful and discard what doesn't suit your style. There is no one right way. Experiment!

Be yourself! Share yourself generously with your audiences and you're assured of success. The world is your oyster — get out there and tell your stories.

Good luck, and above all, have fun, Storyteller!

Storytelling Guilds and Contacts

STORYTELLERS' groups are to be found everywhere. If you are looking for one, we suggest you start with your local library. Should that be unsuccessful, try your State library or Arts Council.

Most storytellers' organisations give a warm welcome to visitors and newcomers. As well as offering the support of like-minded people, they are a great way to enhance and expand your storytelling skills.

Do join a storytelling club. If none exists, form one of your own.

Australia

Storytelling Guild of Australia (NSW) incorporating **Storytellers at the NSW Writers Centre**. Contacts: President Helen McKay on 02 9636 2727, or Berice Dudley on 02 9629 3897. PO Box 76, Pendle Hill, NSW 2145.

This is a very active guild which meets for a full-day workshop every second month: March, May, July, September, November. Specialist presenters in aspects of storytelling offer assistance to members at these workshops. Story cafés, where members can perform are being set up on the alternate months, with an audience of both members and the public. Six issues of the newsletter *Telling Tales*, giving details of Guild activities, are published per year. Members are encouraged to contribute articles or stories to the newsletter, which travels the world.

Storytelling Guild of Australia (Western Australia) Inc. Contacts: President Jenni Woodroffe on 09 9367 4759, or Bookings Officer, Bill Park, 09 9300 0235. PO Box 1170, West Perth, WA 6872.

This guild is very active and vital, with regular informal story-sharing nights, workshops and a series of events titled, 'On the Move', at various venues each month. Their newsletter, *The Spinning Yarn* is published regularly and keeps members abreast of Guild activities.

Storytellers Guild of Australia (ACT) Inc. Contacts: President Catherine Panich on 06 9281 5175, or the Bookings Officer, Eileen Dunstone, on 06 9251 4323. PO Box 420, Dickson, ACT 2602.

This very active, enthusiastic guild holds its meetings at the Belconnen Library in addition to regular story cafés, workshops and events. Their newsletter *Capitales* contains information of events and activities.

Storytelling Guild of Australia (Victorian Branch) Inc. Contact President Gil Di Stefano on 03 9754 3077, PO Box 10, Balwyn, Victoria 3103.

This group meets at the Ashburton Library, 154 High Street, Ashburton, on the first Tuesday of the month. They also hold regular Storytelling Cafés which seem to be a lot of fun. This is an active guild which produces a regular newsletter called *The Harper* detailing all activities and events.

Queensland Storytelling Guild Inc. Contact: Secretary Helen Fitzgerald on (07) 3287 3173. PO Box 2045, Chermside Centre, Queensland 4032.

Through their newsletter, *Scheherazade*, you can learn of their numerous activities and events.

Storytelling Guild of Australia (SA). Contact President Joyce Tyrrell on 08 9337 6144, or Secretary Mildred Bourn on 08 9264 2896. 26 Perseverance Road, Tea Tree Gully, SA 5091. We have recently received the first contact from this guild via their newsletter *The Pied Piper*. The guild meets frequently to present stories and workshops around South Australia.

Other storytelling groups, with varying degrees of activity, are in operation throughout Australia. Contacts which may be of use are:
Tasmania 9/20 Pine Street, West Hobart, Tas 7000.
Northern Territory Try the Northern Territory State Library.
NSW Puppetry Guild Contact: Secretary, Graham Steel, 9 Denning Close, Chipping Norton, NSW 2170.

New Zealand

The New Zealand Guild of Storytellers — *Nga Kaikorero Purakau o Aotearoa.* Contact: President Liz Miller, (Dreamweaver), on 64 03 216 7092. 191 Princes Street, Invercargill, New Zealand; or Treasurer Maureen McEwen on Tel/Fax 64 06 377 0792. 17 Intermediate Street, Masterton, New Zealand.

New Zealand has a very active guild of storytellers spread throughout both islands. The regular newsletter, *Storylines*, keeps members in touch with each other, informed of coming events and workshops. This guild holds an International Festival of Storytelling at Masterton, in the North Island, every alternate year (the next festival will be in October 1996). There are local groups in most parts of the country which may be contacted through the Guild.

USA

The National Storytelling Association (NAPPS) Contact: Secretary on 800 525 4514. PO Box 309, Jonesborough, TN 37659 USA.

With its headquarters in Jonesborough, Tennessee, NAPPS is a connecting point for tellers from all over the USA and internationally. NAPPS offers conferences, workshops and has a strong commitment to the tradition of storytelling. Publishes a monthly newsletter, quarterly magazine, and a National Directory of Storytelling.

The National Story League (Motto: 'Service through Storytelling') Contact: National Story League, c/- Miss Marion Kiligas, 259 E. 41st Street, Norfolk, VA 23504 USA.

Founded in 1903, the League offers workshops, conferences and local support groups. Members give their services free to schools, churches, hospitals and nursing homes.

Storybag — San Diego Contact: Harlynne Geisler on 619 569 9399. c/- Harlynne Geisler, 5361 Javier Street, San Diego, CA 92117-3215 USA.

Harlynne produces the excellent newsletter, *Storybag*, with information about many other storytelling venues and activities in USA.

Junior Storyteller, Contact: Storycraft Publishing, PO Box 205, Masonville, Colorado 80541 USA.

This organisation produces an excellent magazine packed with information for children's groups.

England

Mythos School of Bards, Contact: Ashley Ramsden, Emerson College, Forest Row, East Sussex, England RH 3422282 18SBH 448.

Northern Ireland

Ms Liz Weir, Storyteller in Residence, Anoghill, County Antrim, Northern Ireland, UK RN 18SB.41.

Scotland

Frank McKenna, 2 Quebec Ave, Howden, Livingston, West Lothian, Scotland, EH.54.6BT. Frank recently visited and entertained our guild when in Australia.

Internet

Search for 'storytell' and a large list of sites showing storytelling activities, stories and resources around the world will be displayed — with much available for downloading.

Bibliography

T HIS bibliography lists books we have found helpful in developing our storytelling skills. Some of them may not be easy to acquire. However, since many of them are classics, they are worth chasing. Try your library and request an inter-library loan or, alternatively, hunt around second-hand bookshops, in likely areas.

In Sydney, Berice and I found that the Willoughby Library has the best collection around. Many of the titles were obtained from this library. We've been lucky to meet and talk with some of the authors whom we have profiled. Included are some books that we recommend about the Australian Aboriginal Dreamtime and Spirituality.

Author profiles

Before listing our reccommended books we would like to give a profile of some of the authors. They are:

Philip Cam is the Chair of the Federation of Australasian Philosophy for Children Associations (FAPCA) and a former President of the Philosophy for Children Association of New South Wales, Australia. Dr Cam is senior lecturer in the School of Philosophy at the University of New South Wales. He has published a series of 'thinking stories' for 8-12 year olds with accompanying activity books. These stories 'invite children to question, discuss and explore' different points of view. Stories in Dr Cam's books raise questions about such topics as: appearance and reality; magic and make-believe; mind and body; order in nature; power, freedom and rights; the multicultural society.

Clarissa Pinkola Estés, PhD, is also a Jungian-trained psychoanalyst, cantadora (keeper of the stories) in the Latin tradition, founder of the human-rights organisation, the Guadeloupe Foundation. One of its missions is to broadcast strengthening stories, via short-wave radio, to trouble spots throughout the world. Her book, *Women Who Run With the Wolves*, exposes the deeper meanings and psychology of the stories she presents. It's a must for all readers.

Storyteller, **Gail Herman**, teaches at the 'gifted and talented' education program, Connecticut Confratute (Berice studied with Gail when attending this program). Gail Herman holds Masters degrees in Education in the areas of Theatre and Aesthetics. Her PhD from the University of Connecticut is in Curriculum and Instruction.

Her 'organic' storytelling is a multi-arts, improvisational technique, encouraging imaginative responses from the mind's eye of child audiences. She is affiliated with Frostburg State University and is the Chair of the Visual and Performing Arts Division of the NAGC.

Margaret Read MacDonald holds a PhD in Folklore from Indiana State University. World-travelling storyteller from Seattle (we met her at the International Storytelling Festival at Masterton, in New Zealand in 1994), she has researched stories right back to their earliest sources. We recommend her *Storyteller's Sourcebook*. If you can, get your library to acquire a copy through inter-library loan. As it is a reference book you will only be able to use it at the library.

Margaret MacDonald's books are particularly valuable as she sets out stories in ethnopoetic form — that is, arranged just as they are told, with emphasis and phrasing marked, and lines generously spaced to make it easy for young readers to give a creditable performance when reading aloud (the ideal format for 'reluctant readers'). Her stories are, as she says, 'creations of the tongue, not the pen' having been 'told' into shape by repeated tellings.

Harriet Mason, who sadly died recently, was a Master Storyteller, teacher and marriage, family and child therapist, from Portland, Oregon, who used storytelling to evoke emotions and present alternative ways to feel and behave. Harriet was a member of the Portland, the Seattle and the National Storytelling Guilds. During the time she stayed with Helen in 1995, she shared much information with us. She produced *Every One a Storyteller*, to assist teachers in storytelling for their classrooms. Her set of three tapes entitled 'Telling Makes It So', is also available in transcript form for use by professionals and counsellors.

Diane Wolkstein is the author of 18 books, a teacher and storyteller who has taught mythology and storytelling at universities in New York and California. She has lectured widely across the United States and internationally. All of her books have won awards, some of them multiple awards. Diane toured Australia twice in 1995 presenting performances and workshops in Sydney, Melbourne,

Canberra, Perth and Alice Springs. Her books, *The Magic Orange Tree, Inanna, Queen of Heaven and Earth* and *The First Love Stories* are regarded as classics.

Booklists for the storyteller

Arcodia, Charles. *Stories for Sharing: With themes for discussion starters for teachers and speakers.* E.J. Dwyer, Sydney, 1993.

Baker, Augusta. *Storytelling: Art and Technique.* R.R.Bowker, New York, 1977.

Barton Bob. *Tell Me Another: Storytelling and reading aloud at Home, at School and in the Community.* Pembroke, Ontario, 1986.

Barton Bob and Booth David. *Stories in the Classroom: Storytelling, reading aloud and role-playing with children.* Heinemann, Portsmouth, NH, 1990.

Bauer, Caroline Feller. *New Handbook for Storytellers*, American Library Association, Chicago, 1993.

Blatt, Gloria T. *Once Upon a Folktale: Capturing the folklore process.* Teachers College Press, New York, 1993.

Cam, Philip. *Thinking Stories 1: Philosophical Inquiry for Children.* Hale & Iremonger, Sydney, 1993.

——*Thinking Stories 2: Philosophical Inquiry for Children.* Hale & Iremonger, Sydney, 1994.

——*Thinking Stories 1: Teacher Resource/Activity Book.* Hale & Iremonger, Sydney, 1993.

——*Thinking Stories 2: Teacher Resource/Activity Book.* Hale & Iremonger, Sydney, 1994.

——*Thinking Together: Philosophical Inquiry for the Classroom.* PETA/Hale & Iremonger, Sydney, 1995.

Cassady, Marsh. *Creating Stories for Storytelling.* Resource Publications, San Jose, California, 1991.

——*Storytelling Step by Step.* Resource Publications, San Jose, California, 1990.

Coles, Robert. *The Spiritual Life of Children.* Houghton Mifflin, Boston, 1991.

Colwell, Eileen. *A Storyteller's Choice.* Bodley Head, London, 1963.

Courtney, Bryce. *A Recipe for Dreaming.* William Heinemann, Australia, 1994.

Davis, Donald. *Jack always seeks his fortune.* August House, Little Arkansas, 1992.

Davis, Nancy. *Once Upon a Time: Therapeutic Stories to Heal Abused Children.* Information available through NAPPS, PO Box 309, Jonesborough, Tenn., 37659 USA.

de Vos, Gail. *Storytelling for Young Adults: Technique and Treasury.* Libraries Unlimited, Littleton, Colorado, 1991.

de Wit, Dorothy. *Children's Faces Looking Up: Programme Building for the Storyteller*, American Library Association, Chicago, 1979.

Estés, Clarissa Pinkola. *Women who run with the wolves*. Random House, London, 1993.

——*The Gift of Story*. Ballantine Books, New York, 1993.

Farrell, Catharine. *Storytelling: A Guide For Teachers*. Scholastic, New York, 1991.

Gag, Wanda. *Tales from Grimm*. McCann & Geoghegan, New York, 1981

Griffin, Barbara Budge. *Students as Storytellers: The Long and the Short of Learning a Story*. Medford, Oregon, 1989. Available from author, c/- 10 S. Keeneway Dr., Medford, OR 97504 USA.

Hammond, Catherine. *Stories to Hold an Audience*. Millennium, Sydney, 1995.

Hayes, Barbara and Ingpen, Robert. *Folk Tales and Fables of the World*. David Bateman, Queensland, 1987.

Herman, Gail N. *Storytelling: A Triad in the Arts*. A resource book that blends storytelling with other art forms: music, movement, puppetry and mime. Creative Learning Press Inc., Mansfield Centre, Connecticut, 1986. Available from: PO Box 320, Mansfield Centre, Connecticut, 06250, USA.

Isaacs, Jennifer. *Australian Dreaming*, Lansdowne Press, Adelaide, 1980.

——*Wandjuk Marika: Life Story*. University of Queensland Press, Brisbane, 1995.

Kossoff, David. *Small Town is a World*. Robson Books, London, 1979.

MacDonald, Margaret Read. *The Storyteller's Start-up Book: Finding, learning, and performing folktales*. August House, Little Rock, Arkansas, 1993.

——*Twenty Tellable Tales: Audience Participation Folk Tales*. The H.W. Wilson Company, New York, 1986.

——*Look Back and See: Twenty Lively Tales for Gentle Tellers*. The H.W. Wilson Company, New York, 1991.

——*The Skit Book: 101 Skits from Kids*. Linnet Books/The Shoe String Press, Hamden, Connecticut, 1990.

——*Peace Tales: World Folktales to Tell about*. Linnet Books/The Shoe String Press, Hamden, Connecticut, 1992.

——*Celebrate the World*. The H.W Wilson Company, New York, 1994.

——*When the Lights Go Out: 20 strange and scary tales for children of all ages*. The H.W. Wilson Company, New York, 1988.

MacDonald, Margaret Read & Sturm, Brian. *The Storytellers Source book: A Subject, Title, and Motif-index to Folklore collections for Children*. Neal-Schuman Publishers, Detroit, Michigan, 1982.

Mallan, Kerry. *Children as Storytellers*. PETA, Sydney, 1991.

Mason, Harriet & Watson, Larry. *Every One a Storyteller: Integrating Storytelling into the Curriculum*. Lariat Publications, Portland, Oregon, 1991.

Mason, Harriet. *Telling Makes It So: The Use of Storytelling in Counselling*.

Bibliography

Transcription of the set of three audio-cassette tapes. Lincoln Publishing Inc., Lake Oswego, Oregon, 1994.

Mellon, Nancy. *Storytelling and the Art of Imagination*. Element, Boston, Mass. 1992.

Miller, Patti. *Writing Your Life. A journey of discovery*. Allen & Unwin, Sydney, 1994.

Miller, Teresa. *Joining In: An Anthology of Audience Participation Stories & How to Tell Them*. Yellow Moon Press, Cambridge, Mass., 1988. Available from: PO Box 1316, Cambridge, MA 02238 USA.

Mowaljarlai, David and Malnic, Jutta. *Yorro Yorro: Spirit of the Kimberley*. Magabala Books, Broome, 1993.

Moore, Robyn. *Awakening the Hidden Storyteller: How to build a storytelling tradition in your family*. Shambhala Publications Inc., Boston, 1991.

Nye, Robert. *Classic Folktales From Around the World*. Bracken Books, London, 1994.

Pellowski, Anne. *The World of Storytelling*. Bowker, New York, 1977.

Reneaux, J.J. *Cajun Folktales*. August House, Little Rock, Arkansas, 1992.

Sawyer, Ruth. *Way of the Storyteller*, Penguin, Harmondsworth, 1962. (This book may be hard to get. However, it is a classic)

Shedlock, Marie L. *The Art of the Storyteller*. Dover Publications Inc., New York, 1951.

Shelley, Marshall. *Telling Stories to Children*. Lion Publications, Illinois, 1990.

Shepherd, Aaron. *Savitri: A tale of ancient India*, Albert Whitman, 1992.

Sierra, Judy. *The Flannel Board Storytelling Book*, The H.W.Wilson Company, New York, 1987.

Tashjian, Virginia. *With a Deep Sea Smile. Story Hour Stretches for Large and Small Groups*, Little, Brown & Co., Boston, 1974.

Tooze, Ruth, *Storytelling*. Prentice Hall, New Jersey, 1959

White, William R. *Stories for Telling: A Treasury for Christian Storytellers*, Augsburg, Minneapolis, 1986.

Williamson, Duncan. *Tales of the Sea People,* Congate Press, Edinburgh, 1992.

Wolkstein, Diane. *The Magic Orange Tree and Other Haitian Folktales*, Schocken Books, New York, 1980.

——*The First Love Stories*, Harper Collins, New York, 1991.

——*Inanna, Queen of Heaven and Earth*, Harper Collins, New York, 1983.

——*Esther's Story*, William Morrow, New York, 1995.

——*The Banza*, Dial Books, USA, 1981.

Specialist book series about emotions for children

Anger

Sherwood, Jonathon. *Painting the Fire* (Concept by Liz Farrington), Enchanté Publications, USA, 1995.

Guilt

Sherwood, Jonathon. *Red Poppies For a Little Bird*, (Concept by Liz Farrington), Enchanté Publications, USA, 1995.

Grief

Weil, Jennifer. *And Peter Said Goodbye*, (Concept by Liz Farrington), Enchanté Publications, USA, 1995.

Jealousy

Sherwood, Jonathon. *Tanya and the Green-eyed Monster*, (Concept by Liz Farrington), Enchanté Publications, USA, 1995.

Loneliness

Goldman-Rubin, Susan. *Rainbow Fields*, (Concept by Liz Farrington), Enchanté Publications, USA, 1995.

Fear

McGuire, Leslie. *Nightmare in the Mist*, (Concept by Liz Farrington), Enchanté Publications, USA, 1995.

Hurt

Weil, Jennifer. *William's Gift*, (Concept by Liz Farrington), Enchanté Publications, USA, 1995.

Resources for Storytelling

W E have compiled a short list of places where some resources are available. We suggest you stay alert, as we do, for any other places which you may find when you are travelling around.

Puppets

Marionettes
The Puppet Cottage
77 George Street or Kendall Lane, The Rocks, Sydney, 2000.

Hand Puppets
(Mostly Australian animals) may be obtained wholesale from:

Jozzies Factory
78 Parramatta Road, Stanmore NSW 2048.

RETAIL OUTLETS
Australian Geographic Shops,
Shops Australia-wide.

Chris Rankin's Playhouse: the Kindergarten Toy Shop
152 Clarence Street, Sydney 2001.
Phone: 02 9299 5498

Embraceable Zoo
Level 1, Harbourside, Darling Harbour, Sydney, 2009.

Wombats Too
Level 2, Harbourside, Darling Harbour, Sydney, 2009.

Abracadabra Toys
321 Doncaster Road, Balwyn North, 3104. Phone: 03 9857 8858

Books Illustrated (Open noon to 5pm, Sunday to Thursday)
Gasworks Park, 15 Graham Street, Albert Park, 3206.
(They have a very comprehensive range of insect, bird, fish and animal puppets which are sold accompanied by a story. Write to them for their catalogue.)

Brian Brown
18 Bardoc Crt, Rockingham, 6168. Phone: 09 9592 3060

Finger Puppets
Chris Rankin's Playhouse: the Kindergarten Toy Shop
152 Clarence Street
Sydney, 2001. Phone: 02 9299 5498

Uncle Pete's Toys, Castle Hill
Shop 449, Castle Towers Shopping Centre, Castle Hill 2154. Phone: 02 9680 3493
Shop 88, Warringah Mall, Brookvale 2100. Phone: 02 9938 6533
Shop 32, Roselands Shopping Centre, Roselands 2196. Phone: 02 9759 6722
Shop 31, Stockland Town Centre, Wetherill Park 2164. Phone: 02 9609 7230
CRAFT SHOPS
Berice found some large finger puppets of native animals and birds when hunting round the craft shops in the Hunter Valley. Because we cannot guarantee supply they are not listed. We suggest you investigate the craft shops in your area.

The 'Finger Puppets' sets of puppets and story book are possibly available at your local newsagent or, try Finger Puppet Book Series, Pancake Press, 467 Plummer Street, Port Melbourne 3207.

Puppet patterns
Patterns for making puppets can be found in the craft section of most dressmaking pattern books at all good fabric shops. (e.g. *Butterick, Simplicity, Vogue, Burda*).

Fabrics for puppets
Felt and fake fur of all types, and accessories (such as eyes and whiskers) are available at any comprehensive fabric retailer (especially craft suppliers).

Spotlight Fabrics has retail outlets all over Sydney and stocks a comprehensive supply of these fabrics.

Primitive Instruments and National Costumes

Community Aid Abroad:
- 36 The Corso, Manly 2095. Phone: 02 9977 5391
- Shop CM.05 Centrepoint, Sydney 2000. Phone: 02 9231 4106
- 112 Alinga Street, Canberra 2601. Phone: 06 9247 3272
- 254 Swanston Walk, Melbourne 3000. Phone: 03 9639 4060

- 340 Chapel Street, Prahran 3181. Phone: 03 9510 8232
- Shop 224, Level 2, Myer Centre, Queen St, Brisbane 4000. Phone: 07 9221 4451
- Shop 21, McWhirters Marketplace, Fortitude Valley 4006. Phone: 07 9257 1085
- Shop 2A, Cat & Fiddle Centre, Flinders Mall, Townsville 4810. Phone: 077 9712 946
- Shop 322, Rundle Mall, Adelaide 5000 Phone: 08 9231 0788
- Shop 24, John Martins Place, Charles Street, Adelaide 5000. Phone: 08 9223 1782
- 146 Jetty Road, Glenelg 5045. Phone: 08 9295 5385
- Shop 5, 328 Murray Street, Perth 6000 Phone: 09 9321 3784
- 22 Queen Street, Fremantle, 6160. Phone: 09 9336 3111
- 149A Liverpool Street, Hobart, 7000. Phone: 002 934 6603
- Centreway Arcade, Launceston, 7250. Phone: 003 931 7760

Community Aid Abroad Shop (Oxfam)
Room 101, Lagonda House, 203 Karangahape Road,
Auckland, New Zealand Phone: 64 09 358 1480

Australian Geographic Shops
Shops Australia-wide

Out of Africa Shop
Shop 427, Harbourside, Darling Harbour, Sydney 2009
Phone/fax: 02 9212 7035

Out of Africa Shop
Victoria Park Markets, Victoria Park,
Auckland, New Zealand.

Other Musical Instruments

Good quality musical instruments of all types are available at all good music stores, everywhere. For other instruments, such as good quality tubular bells and chimes, tongue drums and elephant drums, write or phone:

Fascinating Rhythm
PO Box 10–167, Phillipstown,
Christchurch, New Zealand Phone: 64 03 3666 856

Other Storytelling Aids

For magnetic whiteboards, stick-up characters, felt boards, books of plays, dress-up clothes, wafty wings, let's pretend gear. Sets of hand-made finger puppets by Margaret Somerville:

Chris Rankin's Playhouse — the Kindergarten Toy Shop
152 Clarence Street, Sydney, 2001. Phone: 02 9299 5498

Special Educational Resources

Story template pack 1
3 stories, templates or teaching notes.

Story template pack 2
5 rhymes

Stick puppet template pack 1
Templates for 16 farm/zoo animal stick puppets

available from:
Ruth Atkinson, Cheshire Design
4 Oratava Avenue
West Pennant Hills 2125. Phone: 02 982 2152.

Index